TRUE

FACTS

THAT
SOUND
LIKE

Bullsh*t

500 INSANE-BUT-TRUE FACTS THAT WILL
SHOCK AND IMPRESS YOUR FRIENDS

13-Digit ISBN: 9781604336962
10-Digit ISBN: 160433696X

This book may be ordered by mail from the publisher. Please include $5.99 for postage and handling. Please support your local bookseller first!

Books published by Cider Mill Press Book Publishers are available at special discounts for bulk purchases in the United States by corporations, institutions, and other organizations. For more information, please contact the publisher.

Cider Mill Press Book Publishers
"Where good books are ready for press"
PO Box 454
12 Spring Street
Kennebunkport, Maine 04046

Visit us on the Web!
www.cidermillpress.com

Cover design by Melissa Gerber
Interior design by Melissa Gerber
Typography: Adobe Caslon, Eveleth, Capriccio Rough, Festiva Letters, Microbrew, Trade Gothic Bold Condensed
Image Credits: Illustrations by Alex Kalomeris
Vectors and borders are used under official license from Shutterstock.com

Printed in the United States

20 19 18 17 16

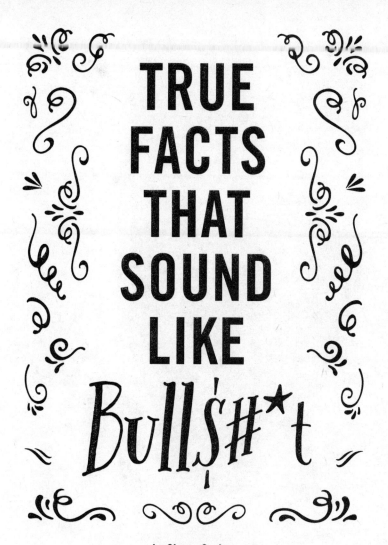

TRUE
FACTS
THAT
SOUND
LIKE
Bull$#*t

by Shane Carley
Illustrated by Alex Kalomeris

CIDER MILL
PRESS

BOOK
PUBLISHERS
KENNEBUNKPORT, MAINE

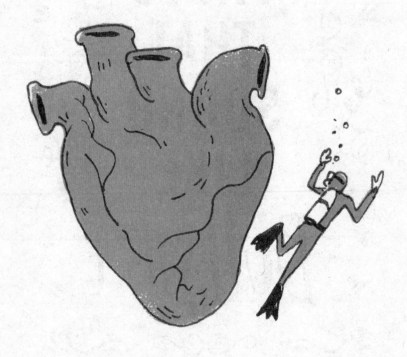

See how big a whale's heart is on page 17.

[CONTENTS]

[Introduction]

The world is a weird place. In fact, the entire universe is a weird place. It always has been. It always will be. There's something comforting about the idea that no matter how much you learn, there will always be new and exciting things to discover.

The joy of discovery is one thing that sets humans apart. We're curious by nature. It's why early explorers set out to discover what lay over the horizon. It's what first led our earliest ancestors to create tools. It's what spurred us to land on the moon. Curiosity has allowed us to do amazing things. Curiosity has moved mountains. And, in its most important achievement to date, curiosity is what made you pick up this book.

You'll be glad you did! Discovering new things doesn't have to mean cataloging a new species of antelope or documenting an unnamed asteroid. Sometimes it's just about learning new things and exposing yourself to new ideas. Discovering isn't always big. Sometimes, it's personal. And whether your interest lies in weird animals, crazy plants, mind-blowing athletic achievements, or unbelievable discoveries light-years from Earth, you'll be shocked and amazed by what you discover within these pages.

STRANGE BUT TRUE
Nature Facts

Nature can be cool. It can be scary. It can be wonderful. But most of all, it can be unbelievable. Think about it—how many everyday facts that we take for granted would sound crazy if you were learning them for the first time?

Redwood trees can grow to almost 300 feet tall and 30 feet wide.
There are 100,000,000,000 stars in our galaxy alone.
People drive hundreds of miles to watch leaves die.
The platypus *exists*.

In this chapter, we're going to dig a little deeper and examine some truly wild facts about plants, animals, and all kinds of natural phenomena. Because just when you think you know everything there is to know about nature, someone comes along and tells you that hippopotamus sweat is pink.

1. HIPPOPOTAMUS SWEAT IS PINK.

This isn't entirely accurate—hippo sweat comes out clear, just as ours does. But the hippopotamus secretes hipposudoric acid, which has a red tint to it, and quickly turns hippo sweat to a shade of pink dark enough that it is sometimes mistaken for blood. Commonly referred to as "blood sweat," this acidic coating helps protect the hippo from both sun damage and harmful bacteria.

A POPULAR ONLINE RUMOR SUGGESTS THAT HIPPOPOTAMUS MILK IS PINK, RATHER THAN SWEAT. INTERESTING AS THAT WOULD BE, IT IS SIMPLY NOT TRUE.

2. KANGAROOS PERFORM ADOPTIONS.

Humans aren't the only species to perform adoptions. Kangaroos have been known to accidentally abandon their young, only to have them raised by other kangaroos. Sometimes kangaroos even voluntarily swap babies.

3. KILLER WHALES EAT DEER.

Most notably in Alaska, killer whales, or orcas, have been known to prey on deer that decide to take a dip in the water. Some have even been known to regurgitate fish onto the surface of the water to lure in seagulls, too.

4. WOOLLY MAMMOTHS WERE STILL AROUND DURING THE CONSTRUCTION OF THE PYRAMIDS.

The last of the woolly mammoths only died approximately 4,000 years ago, which just so happens to be around the same time the Great Pyramid was built. Imagine what the ancient Egyptians would have thought if they had been able to see the mammoths!

5. THE *TYRANNOSAURUS REX* LIVED CLOSER TO OUR TIME THAN TO THE *STEGOSAURUS*.

6. THE *STEGOSAURUS* IS OLDER THAN GRASS.

What we now know as "grasses" did not evolve until well into the Cretaceous period, which began 145 million years ago. The *Stegosaurus* roamed the earth during the Jurassic period, 155 to 150 million years ago, and instead consumed mosses, ferns, and other fauna.

7. ABOUT 80% OF ALL INDIVIDUAL ANIMALS ON EARTH ARE NEMATODES.

8. THE *TYRANNOSAURUS REX* IS ESTIMATED TO HAVE HAD A BITE FORCE OF ALMOST 13,000 POUNDS PER SQUARE INCH.

AMONG DINOSAURS, ONLY THE *C. MEGALODON* IS ESTIMATED TO TOP THE *T. REX*'S BITE FORCE, COMING IN AT AN ASTONISHING 41,000 PSI.

That's almost equal to the average body weight of an adult *T. rex*! The strongest animals today (saltwater crocodiles) are estimated to have a bite force of around 5,000 pounds per square inch (PSI), though some speculate that the bite force of the orca whale could be significantly higher.

9. MAGGOTS ARE STILL USED TO CLEAN WOUNDS.

In fact, as recently as 2004, the U.S. Food and Drug Administration permitted the production and marketing of maggots for limited use as a "medical device."

10. BEFORE DINOSAURS, THERE WERE FUNGI. GIANT, 26-FOOT-TALL FUNGI, TO BE PRECISE.

These giant fungi were known as *Prototaxites*, and could grow up to twenty-six feet tall and three feet wide. They existed from approximately 420 to 370 million years ago.

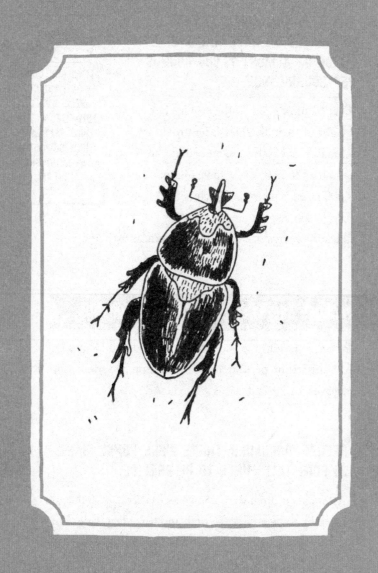

· 11 ·

ABOUT **25%** OF
ALL LIFE ON EARTH
CONSISTS OF BEETLES.
THAT INCLUDES PLANTS.

12. LIGHTNING CAN EXPLODE TREES.

Most trees (especially dying or rotting trees) contain quite a bit of water. When lightning strikes a tree, much of that water is immediately raised to boiling temperatures, turning it to steam and causing a spike in pressure that can cause the tree to explode.

13. THERE IS EVIDENCE THAT CERTAIN SPECIES OF BABOONS KEEP DOGS AS PETS.

14. ANGLERFISH REPRODUCE BY FUSING THEMSELVES WITH THE OPPOSITE SEX IN A PARASITE-LIKE RELATIONSHIP.

Because anglerfish live at the very bottom of the ocean, it can be difficult for members of the species to find each other. Rather than rely on traditional reproduction, the much larger females of the species fuse with the tiny male anglerfish. They can "mate" in this way with up to six males at once, ensuring a constant supply of sperm for reproduction.

15. FOR EVERY HUMAN ON THE PLANET EARTH, THERE ARE ABOUT 1,600,000 MILLION ANTS.

Obviously, we can only estimate. Some say more, some say less, but 1,600,000 million is the approximate middle ground between most estimates.

16. WE THINK OF TOMATOES AS BEING FROM ITALY, BUT THEY WERE FIRST GROWN IN SOUTH AMERICA.

17. TARSIERS HAVE EYES AS BIG AS THEIR BRAIN.

That is to say, each eye is the same size as a tarsier's brain. These adorable primates actually have eyes so big that they cannot move in their sockets. Instead, their necks have evolved to allow their heads to swivel much like an owl's.

18. BANANAS ARE TECHNICALLY BERRIES. STRAWBERRIES AND RASPBERRIES ARE NOT.

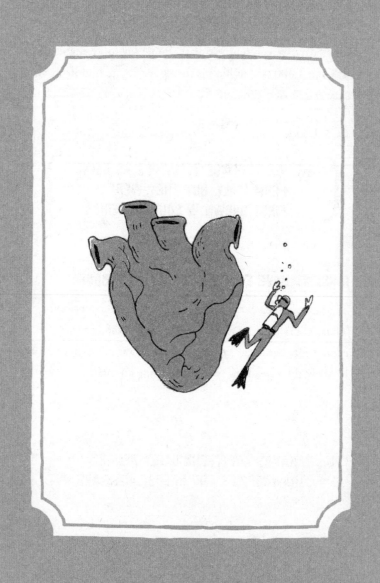

· 19 ·

YOU COULD SWIM THROUGH THE VEINS OF A BLUE WHALE.

It may sound crazy, but it's true. The average blue whale has a heart that is approximately the size of a car, so it should come as no surprise that it has massive veins to match.

20. THERE IS A SPECIES OF ANT THAT SELF-DESTRUCTS AS A DEFENSE MECHANISM.

The *Camponotus saundersi* species of ant can cause two mandibular glands to explode when it is losing a fight. The glands are filled with a corrosive and sticky substance that can immobilize its attackers and save other members of its colony.

21. ALMOST 90% OF HUMANS ON EARTH LIVE IN THE NORTHERN HEMISPHERE.

22. WHALES EVOLVED FROM DEER.

Okay, this one is a little fudged. But the earliest known ancestor of today's whales is the *Indohyus*, which was a small, deer-like creature that existed 48 million years ago. Over time, the creature and its descendants became increasingly aquatic, eventually resulting in the whales we see today.

23. THE AVERAGE WEIGHT OF A CUMULUS CLOUD IS 1.1 MILLION POUNDS.

Although they are light and fluffy and float high in the air, clouds are actually extremely heavy. People sometimes forget that they are actually made up of water vapor, and water has quite a bit of heft to it!

24. ALTHOUGH THE EARTH IS 70% WATER, JUST 1% OF IT IS CONSIDERED DRINKABLE.

25. BLUE WHALES CAN BE HEARD FROM OVER 500 MILES AWAY.

Granted, human ears won't be able to pick up the sound. But other blue whales (or very sensitive audio equipment) can hear them!

26. MONOGAMOUS ANIMALS INCLUDE BEAVERS, WOLVES, AND SWANS.

27. SOME SNAKES CAN FLY.

Well, not exactly "fly." But the *Chrysopelea*, a genus known as the "flying snakes," can leap from trees and glide distances of over 300 feet!

28. DOGS CAN READ HUMAN BODY LANGUAGE.

When people say "dogs can smell fear," in a way it's true! They can also sense happiness, sadness, and other emotions simply by reading human body language.

• 29 •

PLATYPUSES AREN'T JUST WEIRD. THEY CAN POISON YOU.

Platypuses are one of just a few mammals to produce their own venom, which is injected via barbs on the male's hind legs. This venom is highly toxic, and, while it probably won't kill you, can cause an incredible amount of pain.

30. VAMPIRE BATS REALLY DO DRINK BLOOD.

It's not just a myth! Vampire bats have a diet based entirely on blood (typically cow's blood).

31. AN OSTRICH COULD KICK YOU TO DEATH.

In fact, an ostrich's kick is so strong that they have been known to kill lions with a single, well-placed kick.

32. PANDAS TYPICALLY NEED TO CONSUME AT LEAST TWENTY-SIX POUNDS OF BAMBOO PER DAY TO SURVIVE.

33. THE FEMALE PRAYING MANTIS ISN'T THE ONLY INSECT TO EAT ITS MATE.

Many spiders, including the tarantula, also consume (or attempt to consume) their partners after mating.

34. ALLIGATORS ARE TRULY PREHISTORIC PREDATORS.

Alligators have been around, in more or less their current form, for over 150 million years. That's a long time!

35. THERE IS A SPECIES OF TURTLE THAT CAN BREATHE THROUGH ITS BUTT.

The white-throated snapping turtle of Australia has earned the nickname "the bum-breathing turtle" in honor the fact that it can intake most of the oxygen it needs through its rear end.

36. PUFFINS SET ASIDE AN AREA IN THEIR HOMES AS A "BATHROOM."

37. THERE IS A SPECIES OF JELLYFISH THAT IS FUNCTIONALLY IMMORTAL.

Found in the Mediterranean Sea and off the coast of Japan, the "immortal jellyfish" can, in theory, continue to regenerate its cells indefinitely (although in practice, they are usually eaten by predators).

38. BABY SEA TURTLES CAN COMMUNICATE WITH EACH OTHER BEFORE THEY HATCH.

· 39 ·

NORWAY KNIGHTED A PENGUIN.

Yes, you read that right. In 2008, King Harold V of Norway approved the knighthood of Sir Nils Olav, a penguin from the Edinburgh Zoo in Scotland that was adopted by a Norwegian military unit.

40. CROWS CAN ACTUALLY RECOGNIZE HUMAN FACES.

It's not just dogs that recognize people. Studies have shown that crows can recognize human faces, and even pick them out of a crowd.

41. OCTOPUSES HAVE INCREDIBLE PROBLEM-SOLVING SKILLS.

Many have been known to slip from their aquarium tanks to eat other exhibits. Others have managed to escape captivity entirely! Aristotle, who famously thought that octopuses were stupid, would be shocked.

43. ALGAE AND PLANKTON PRODUCE MORE OXYGEN THAN TREES.

42. THERE IS A SPECIES OF OCTOPUS WITH DETACHABLE SEXUAL ORGANS.

The male argonaut octopus mates by detaching its sexual organ and flinging it toward the female. It then makes its way inside the female to fertilize her eggs.

44. DESPITE NOT EXISTING, THE UNICORN IS THE "NATIONAL ANIMAL" OF SCOTLAND.

45. ONE OF THE MOST VENOMOUS CREATURES ON EARTH IS A SNAIL.

The geographic cone snail produces venom that paralyzes its prey instantly. After all, if the venom took too much time to take effect, the slow-moving snail might never catch up to its prey.

46. UNTIL JUST A FEW HUNDRED YEARS AGO, ALL OF THE ANTS ON EARTH LIKELY OUTWEIGHED ALL OF THE HUMANS ON EARTH.

Humans have proven to be prolific procreators, and within the last 300 years or so the human population has exploded. Of course, we humans are also getting heavier...

47. ZEBRAS AND TIGERS EACH HAVE A UNIQUE STRIPE PATTERN—MUCH LIKE A HUMAN FINGERPRINT.

• 48 •

THERE ARE MORE TREES ON EARTH THAN THERE ARE STARS IN THE MILKY WAY.

Astronomers estimate that there are about 200 to 400 billion stars in the Milky Way, while scientists say Earth contains 3 trillion trees.

49. COFFEE COMES FROM CHERRIES.

The coffee beans that we all know and love are actually the pit (and seed) of a cherry-like fruit that grows from the coffee plant.

50. MOST OF THE SOIL ON CANADA'S PRINCE EDWARD ISLAND IS A VIBRANT, BRICK RED COLOR.

51. THE FIRST PEOPLE TO MEASURE MOUNT EVEREST LIED ABOUT HOW TALL IT WAS.

Their measurement was exactly 29,000 feet—but the surveyors thought no one would believe that it came to such an exact measurement, so they added two more feet to the total. Today, the official height is listed as 29,029 feet.

52. IT WOULD TAKE OVER ONE MILLION MOSQUITOES TO DRAIN A HUMAN BEING OF BLOOD.

53. YOU WERE ONCE A DISEMBODIED ANUS.

When humans develop in the womb, one of the very first things to form is the anus.

54. THE AVERAGE 200-POUND HUMAN CARRIES BETWEEN TWO AND SIX POUNDS OF BACTERIA.

55. YOU MAY KNOW THAT COWS HAVE FOUR STOMACHS, BUT DID YOU KNOW THAT OCTOPUSES HAVE THREE HEARTS?

56. CROCODILES MAY LOOK LIKE LIZARDS, BUT THEY ARE ACTUALLY MORE CLOSELY RELATED TO BIRDS.

This should come as no surprise to anyone who knows that birds are directly descended from dinosaurs.

57. SHARKS ARE OLDER THAN TREES.

"Trees" as we know them are only about 350 million years old. Sharks, on the other hand, date back 400 million years.

• 58 •

TRUE OR FALSE: THERE IS AN OCTOPUS NICKNAMED THE "BAMBI OCTOPUS."

False. But there is a miniature octopus nicknamed the Dumbo Octopus, due to the ear-like appearance of their fins.

59. CHANCES ARE, THERE ARE MORE BACTERIA CELLS IN YOUR BODY THAN HUMAN CELLS—SOME SCIENTISTS BELIEVE AS MANY AS TEN TIMES MORE.

60. YOU CAN GENERALLY TELL THE COLOR OF A CHICKEN'S EGGS BY THE COLOR OF ITS EARS.

61. THE "LOUDEST PENIS" IN THE ANIMAL KINGDOM BELONGS TO THE LESSER WATER BOATMAN INSECT.

Measured at 99.2 decibels, the sound was so loud that scientists at first didn't believe their instruments were working properly. In fact, the lesser water boatman is the loudest animal on earth relative to its body size.

62. A CHICKEN ONCE SURVIVED ALMOST TWO YEARS AFTER HAVING ITS HEAD CUT OFF.

Mike the Headless Chicken, as he would come to be known, survived when the axe stroke missed his jugular vein and most of his brain stem.

MIKE THE HEADLESS CHICKEN TOURED THE COUNTRY AND BECAME FAMOUS, THOUGH HE HAD TO BE FED THROUGH AN EYEDROPPER.

63. TRUE OR FALSE: BUTTERFLIES TASTE WITH THEIR FEET.

True. That's where their taste sensors are!

64. TRUE OR FALSE: GOATS HAVE ACCENTS.

True. Goats in different areas of the world bleat in ways that are recognizably distinctive to that region.

65. TRUE OR FALSE: REINDEER HAVE RED EYES.

False. Actually, reindeer eyes change color throughout the year. In the winter, they turn blue. This helps them see in lower light.

66. TRUE OR FALSE: WHEN HONEY BEES FIND A POSSIBLE PLACE FOR A NEST, THEY PERFORM SOMETHING CALLED A "WAGGLE DANCE."

True! This is how they indicate to other bees that they want to nest there.

67. TRUE OR FALSE: BEAVERS USED TO BE THE SIZE OF BEARS.

True. Like many animals, beavers became smaller as they evolved.

• 68 •

TRUE OR FALSE: BEAVERS' BUTTS TASTE LIKE VANILLA.

True. Well…sort of. Beavers
secrete a substance from their
anal glands that is used in
artificial vanilla flavoring. Yum.

69. IN WARM CLIMATES, HUMANS ARE THE BEST ENDURANCE RUNNERS IN THE ANIMAL KINGDOM.

70. TRUE OR FALSE: HUMANS ARE THE ONLY ANIMALS TO PERFORM ORAL SEX ON EACH OTHER.

False! Plenty of animals, including bears, lions, and monkeys, perform oral sex (although none have been observed to 69).

71. TRUE OR FALSE: SQUIRRELS VOMIT UP 50% OF THE FOOD THEY INGEST.

False. Actually, squirrels are completely incapable of vomiting, as are most rodents.

72. TRUE OR FALSE: DOLPHINS GIVE EACH OTHER NAMES.

True. They communicate with each other and even call each other by "name."

73. TRUE OR FALSE: THE HORNED LIZARD CAN SHOOT BLOOD FROM ITS EYES AS A DEFENSE MECHANISM.

True. In fact, they can squirt blood up to three feet!

74. TRUE OR FALSE: DOLPHINS ARE AMONG THE GENTLEST CREATURES IN THE ANIMAL KINGDOM.

False. In fact, dolphins have been known to not only sexually assault other dolphins…but humans as well.

75. TRUE OR FALSE: THE DADDY LONGLEG IS ACTUALLY ONE OF THE DEADLIEST SPIDERS ON EARTH, BUT ITS FANGS CANNOT PENETRATE HUMAN SKIN.

False on both counts.

76. TRUE OR FALSE: PEOPLE STANDING ON THE EQUATOR ARE MOVING AT ABOUT 2,000 MILES PER HOUR.

False. The earth rotates at a speed of about 1,000 MPH. On the other hand, if you're standing on the North Pole, you're essentially spinning in place.

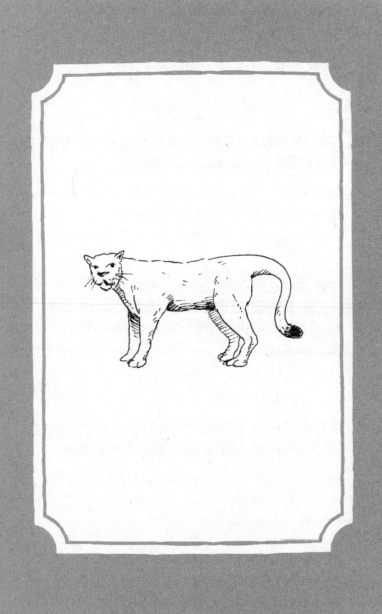

• 77 •

TRUE OR FALSE:
FEMALE LIONS
ARE THE PRIMARY
HUNTERS.

True. Typical men…so lazy.

78. TRUE OR FALSE: A GROUP OF RHINOCEROSES IS CALLED A "CRASH."

True.

79. TRUE OR FALSE: ANTS HAVE SIX LUNGS.

False. Actually, ants have no lungs!

80. TRUE OR FALSE: THERE ARE AREAS ON EARTH WITH LESS GRAVITY THAN OTHERS.

True. Weird as it sounds, the Earth does not have evenly distributed density, which means some areas have slightly less gravity than others.

81. TRUE OR FALSE: EARTH'S MAGNETIC POLES CAN MOVE.

True. In fact, the poles slowly drift over time and flip every few hundred thousand years. And we're due for it to happen again!

82. TRUE OR FALSE: IF WE REMOVED EVERY BOAT, SHIP, AND SUBMARINE FROM THE OCEANS, THE SEA LEVEL WOULD FALL ABOUT SIX INCHES.

False. The sea level would actually fall by only the width of a human hair.

83. TRUE OR FALSE: FEMALE KOALAS HAVE TWO VAGINAS.

True, as crazy as it sounds!

84. TRUE OR FALSE: SOME ANIMALS CAN SMELL WATER.

True...apparently. Elephants can smell water from miles away, although it is possible that they have simply learned to detect the smell of animals and plants frequently found in and around water.

85. TRUE OR FALSE: CATS WERE THE FIRST ANIMALS DOMESTICATED BY HUMANS.

False. That honor goes to dogs, which were domesticated over 12,000 years ago. Even goats predate cats, having been domesticated 10,000 years ago.

DOMESTIC CATS DATE BACK JUST 4,000 YEARS OR SO.

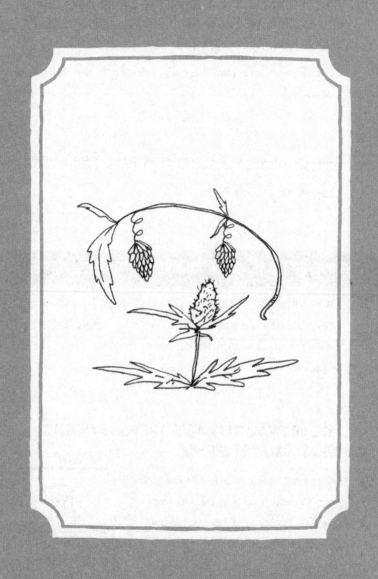

· 86 ·

**TRUE OR FALSE:
MARIJUANA AND THE
HOPS IN YOUR BEER
COME FROM THE SAME
PLANT FAMILY.**

True. The Cannabaceae family
also contains plants known as
hackberries.

87. TRUE OR FALSE: A BLIND CHAMELEON DEFAULTS TO A GREEN COLOR TO BLEND IN WITH THE PLANTS IN ITS NATURAL HABITAT.

False. Even if a chameleon is blind, its color changing camouflage still works!

88. TRUE OR FALSE: SEA STARS (STARFISH) HAVE JUST ONE EYE—RIGHT IN THE CENTER OF THEIR BODIES.

False. Actually, sea stars have an eye at the end of each arm.

89. TRUE OR FALSE: THE OLDEST TREE IN THE WORLD DATES BACK TO THE TIME OF THE DINOSAURS.

False. Although trees have a long life span, the oldest known trees date back just a few thousand years, well short of the dinosaurs.

90. TRUE OR FALSE: WHEN A WORKER BEE MATES WITH THE QUEEN BEE, ITS PENIS EXPLODES.

True. You can even hear it pop if you listen close.

91. TRUE OR FALSE: A FLATWORM CAN LAUNCH A PROJECTILE FROM ITS ANUS WHEN IT HUNTS.

False. But it can use its penis as a weapon!

92. TRUE OR FALSE: DURING MATING SEASON, LIONS CAN HAVE SEX DOZENS OF TIMES EVERY DAY.

True.

93. TRUE OR FALSE: THE HAIRY FROG IS ALSO KNOWN AS THE "HORROR FROG" DUE TO THE HIGH-PITCHED SHRIEK IT EMITS WHEN THREATENED.

False. The "horror frog" is so named because it intentionally breaks the bones in its leg to create weaponized spurs.

94. TRUE OR FALSE: THE ANIMAL WITH THE LONGEST HIBERNATION PERIOD IS A FROG.

True. The wood frog has been observed to hibernate for up to seven months! No other animal is known to hibernate for even six months.

• 95 •

TRUE OR FALSE: THE AFRICAN BOTTLE TREE IS UNIQUE DUE TO ITS ABILITY TO SURVIVE ON JUST ONE TEASPOON OF WATER PER MONTH.

False. Although estimates vary, the bottle tree is believed to hold hundreds (or even thousands) of liters of water at a time!

96. TRUE OR FALSE: THE SCALLOP IS THE ONLY MOLLUSK THAT IS COMPLETELY BLIND.

False. In fact, scallops have over a dozen eyes all along the edge of their shells!

97. TRUE OR FALSE: ELEPHANTS CAN JUMP HIGHER THAN ANY OTHER ANIMAL.

False. Elephants actually can't jump at all.

98. TRUE OR FALSE: ELECTRIC EELS ARE ACTUALLY MISNAMED, AND THE "SHOCK" THAT THEY PRODUCE IS ACTUALLY DUE TO A TOXIC VENOM THAT THEY SECRETE.

False. Electric eels really are electric! They can discharge over 500 volts of electricity at once!

99. TRUE OR FALSE: A STRAWBERRY ISN'T REALLY A FRUIT...IT'S A FLOWER.

True! Technically, the little yellow seeds on the outside of the strawberry are its "fruit," while the flesh itself is part of the flower.

PEOPLE SAY BIRDS ARE THE CLOSEST THING TO DINOSAURS, AND THEY'RE RIGHT! BIRDS BELONG TO THE CLADE *DINOSAURIA*, MEANING THAT THEY SHARE A COMMON ANCESTOR WITH THE DINOSAURS.

[OUT-OF-THIS-WORLD Space Facts]

When it comes to space, there's not much that ISN'T crazy. Remember the first time you heard about a black hole? Didn't that blow your mind? It turns out that there are plenty of other space facts out there that will blow your mind just as much.

We won't just stick to our own solar system, either—although there are probably enough facts about Jupiter alone to build an entirely new book around! No, we'll learn about planets, comets, stars, quasars, and even the empty vacuum of space. That's the great thing about space: it goes on and on forever, meaning that there will never be any shortage of crazy new discoveries!

1. EVERY PLANET IN THE SOLAR SYSTEM COULD FIT IN THE SPACE BETWEEN EARTH AND THE MOON.

Yes, even if you count Pluto.

2. IF THE SUN SUDDENLY DISAPPEARED, EARTH WOULD CONTINUE ALONG ITS ORBITAL PATH FOR EIGHT MINUTES.

Nothing can travel faster than light—and that includes gravity. It would take eight minutes for the gravitational effect of the missing sun to reach Earth.

3. ONE DAY ON VENUS IS LONGER THAN ONE YEAR ON VENUS.

One day (a complete rotation) on Venus is equal to approximately 243 Earth days. Its year (a trip around the sun) lasts 224 Earth days. This means that the planet travels all the way around the sun before finishing a complete rotation!

4. IC 1101, THE LARGEST GALAXY EVER DISCOVERED, IS 60 TIMES THE SIZE OF THE MILKY WAY.

IC 1101 is a staggering 6,000,000 light-years in diameter! For comparison's sake, the Milky Way is just 100,000 light-years across. The galaxy is estimated to contain upwards of one trillion stars.

· 5 ·

VENUS SPINS BACKWARDS. AND NO ONE KNOWS WHY!

While the rest of the planets in our solar system spin counter-clockwise, Venus spins in a clockwise "retrograde" rotation. While there are a few theories about why this is the case, no one can yet say for sure.

6. *ALIEN* WAS RIGHT: IN SPACE, NO ONE CAN HEAR YOU SCREAM.

What we hear as sound is vibration traveling through the molecules in the air. Since space is a vacuum, there are no molecules to vibrate.

7. THE FOOTPRINTS THAT OUR ASTRONAUTS HAVE LEFT ON THE MOON WILL PROBABLY NEVER GO AWAY.

Because the moon has no atmosphere, it has no wind. The only way for the moon's dust to be disturbed is probably via impact events.

8. THE LARGEST MOUNTAIN IN THE SOLAR SYSTEM IS NEARLY THREE TIMES THE SIZE OF MOUNT EVEREST. OH, AND IT'S A VOLCANO.

Olympus Mons, the tallest peak on Mars, stands a towering 85,000 feet above the Martian plains.

9. BECAUSE OF IRREGULARITIES IN EARTH'S ROTATION, A "LEAP SECOND" OCCASIONALLY HAS TO BE INSERTED TO THE COORDINATED UNIVERSAL TIME.

10. THE LARGEST KNOWN STAR HAS A VOLUME THAT IS ALMOST 7 BILLION TIMES GREATER THAN THE SUN.

UY Scuti is estimated to have a solar radius 2,708 times greater than the sun, and if it were superimposed over our solar system, it would engulf everything within at least the orbit of Jupiter. Some scientists believe that it may be even larger, but this seems to be the most generally accepted estimate.

11. THE INTERNATIONAL SPACE STATION HAS A MOVIE THEATER.

Well, not exactly a movie theater, but it does have a zero gravity projector designed to let astronauts watch movies. Naturally, movies that have been watched on the screen include films like *Gravity* and *Star Trek*.

12. THE MILKY WAY CONTAINS CLOUDS OF ALCOHOL BILLIONS OF MILES WIDE.

Methanol and ethyl alcohol are natural forms of alcohol, and massive clouds of them have formed in space!

13. THERE ARE STARS THAT ARE SO COLD YOU COULD TOUCH THEM.

If, you know, the gravity didn't crush you first.

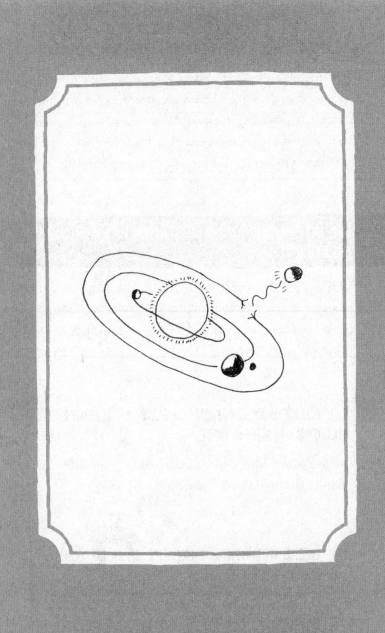

· 14 ·

**PLANETS CAN BE
EJECTED FROM
SOLAR SYSTEMS.**

15. SPACE LIGHTNING EXISTS.

You probably thought they made that up for *Star Trek*, right? Nope. Turns out lightning can occur naturally smack dab in outer space. Except this lightning is caused by black holes and can stretch longer than the width of the entire Milky Way.

16. THE SUN MAKES UP OVER 99% OF THE SOLAR SYSTEM'S MASS.

17. YOU ARE TALLER IN SPACE THAN YOU ARE ON EARTH.

This one actually makes logical sense: gravity isn't pulling you downward and compressing your spine, so you gain a little bit of height!

18. THE NORTH STAR HAS CHANGED...AND WILL CHANGE AGAIN.

Stars move. The current "North Star" is Polaris, but before Polaris it was Thuban. In about 12,000 years, the star closest to our northern pole will be Vega.

19. THERE IS A PLANET MADE OF DIAMOND.

Much of the mass of 55 Cancri e comes from crystalized diamond. At one point, scientists believed that the majority of the planet's mass might be carbon (the element from which diamonds are made), but recent studies have scaled back those estimates. At the very least, the planet appears to have a thick layer of diamond near its surface.

20. THERE ARE STRUCTURES IN SPACE SO BIG THAT THEY DEFY OUR UNDERSTANDING OF PHYSICS.

The Hercules-Corona Borealis Great Wall, for example, is a massive galactic structure that appears to be larger than what scientists previously considered the upper limit for such structures.

21. THERE IS AN OBJECT IN SPACE CALLED THE "GREAT ATTRACTOR." AND WE HAVE NO IDEA WHAT IT IS.

It is classified as a "gravitational anomaly," and all we can say for sure is that it is moving…and it is taking a lot of galaxies and galaxy clusters with it.

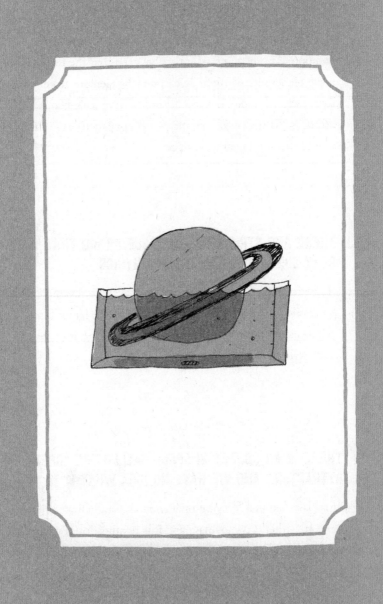

• 22 •

SATURN WOULD FLOAT ON WATER.

You probably know that Saturn is a gas giant. But did you know that the planet is less dense than water? If you could find a pool big enough to fit the entire planet, Saturn would float happily on top of it.

23. CONSTELLATIONS ARE RATIFIED BY THE INTERNATIONAL ASTRONOMICAL UNION.

It sounds crazy, but there is actually a list of "officially recognized" constellations. Some formerly well-known constellations have been dropped from the list over the years!

24. IF THE ANDROMEDA GALAXY (OUR CLOSEST NEIGHBOR) WAS BRIGHTER, IT WOULD APPEAR LARGER THAN THE FULL MOON IN OUR SKY.

25. SPACE SMELLS LIKE STEAK.

Obviously you can't smell space (since there is no air), but, when astronauts return, they often find that their equipment smells like cooked steak.

26. IN ORDER FOR EARTH TO BECOME A BLACK HOLE, ITS ENTIRE MASS WOULD HAVE TO BE COMPRESSED INTO A SPACE LESS THAN AN INCH IN DIAMETER.

27. WE ALMOST NUKED THE MOON.

Back in the 1950s, the U.S. Air Force considered launching a nuclear missile at the moon as a show of superiority (the blast would have likely been visible from Earth).

28. THE MOON ISN'T EARTH'S ONLY NATURAL SATELLITE.

There are actually quite a few asteroids and other small bodies that have been discovered orbiting the earth, but none of them are nearly large enough to be considered noteworthy.

29. SCIENTISTS THEORIZE THAT "WHITE HOLES" MAY EXIST. THEY WOULD BE (ESSENTIALLY) THE OPPOSITE OF BLACK HOLES.

30. THERE IS A STORM ON JUPITER THREE TIMES THE SIZE OF EARTH.

You've probably heard of Jupiter's Great Red Spot. But did you know that it is actually a storm that has been raging for hundreds of years and could fit the entire Earth inside it three times over?

· 31 ·

BUZZ ALDRIN HAPPILY CLAIMS TO BE THE FIRST MAN TO PEE ON THE MOON.

It seems unlikely that anyone is ever going to contest that claim.

32. THERE ARE VAMPIRE STARS.

Sometimes, in a binary system (two stars orbiting each other, or one orbiting the other), the more massive star will begin to draw energy from the weaker star, sucking its hydrogen away and shrinking the weaker star.

33. THERE ARE GALAXIES MOVING AWAY FROM US FASTER THAN THE SPEED OF LIGHT.

Nothing can move faster than the speed of light. But because the fabric of the universe is also expanding, some galaxies moving away from us are receding faster than the speed of light.

34. IT TAKES 200 MILLION YEARS FOR THE SUN TO MAKE ONE ORBIT AROUND THE GALACTIC CENTER.

35. THE SUN RISES AND SETS ON THE INTERNATIONAL SPACE STATION AROUND 15 TIMES A DAY.

The ISS orbits Earth once every 90 minutes or so, so they see the sun come over the horizon around 15 times a day!

36. SOME SCIENTISTS THINK WE MAY HAVE FOUND AN ALIEN MEGASTRUCTURE ORBITING A DISTANT STAR.

The star KIC 8462852 has been found to brighten and dim periodically, leading some eager scientists to optimistically speculate that an alien structure is periodically blocking light, though many believe there are other, better explanations.

37. YOU CAN'T WHISTLE IN SPACE.

More specifically, you can't whistle in a spacesuit. There just isn't enough air pressure to create the necessary conditions!

38. AS FAR AS OFFICIAL RECORDS ARE CONCERNED, NO ONE HAS EVER HAD SEX IN SPACE.

But who really knows for sure?

39. ANIMALS THAT HAVE BEEN TO SPACE INCLUDE NOT JUST DOGS, CATS, AND MONKEYS, BUT ALSO FROGS AND LITERAL GUINEA PIGS.

40. BOOMERANGS WORK IN SPACE.

Astronauts on the International Space Station have proven that a boomerang will return to them in microgravity—just don't try throwing one in a total vacuum or you'll never see it again!

41. ASTRONAUTS CAN GROW FOOD IN SPACE. DIRTY UNDERWEAR HELPS.

Astronauts have to reuse clothing a lot (there's no laundry, after all!), and astronaut Don Pettit decided that the extra "nutrients" in his dirty underwear might help his plants grow. He was right!

THE INSULATION FROM THE UNDERWEAR ALSO HELPED KEEP THE SEEDS WARM ENOUGH TO GROW.

42. METAL FUSES TOGETHER IN SPACE.

This is called "cold welding," and is actually used in some manufacturing processes on Earth. In space, though, it's important to keep pieces of the same type of metal apart.

43. THE ARDBEG DISTILLERY HAS AGED WHISKY IN SPACE!

Naturally, they named it "Supernova."

44. NEUTRON STARS CAN SPIN OVER 700 TIMES PER SECOND.

Neutron stars are among the densest objects in the universe, and a lot of force is generated by their rapid motion!

45. TRUE OR FALSE: RUSSIAN COSMONAUTS USED TO CARRY WEAPONS IN SPACE IN CASE THEY LANDED IN THE WILDERNESS.

True! Knives, machetes, and even guns have all been reportedly carried by Russian cosmonauts for protection from terrestrial wildlife.

46. TRUE OR FALSE: THERE ARE ABOUT TWO BILLION GALAXIES IN THE OBSERVABLE UNIVERSE.

False. Scientists estimate that there are one hundred billion galaxies in the observable universe alone. Beyond that... who knows!

47. TRUE OR FALSE: ASTRONAUTS CAN FEEL THROUGH THE FINGERTIPS OF THEIR SPACESUIT.

True! Well, mostly. Spacesuits contain silicone fingertips, which allow the astronauts to experience some sense of touch rather than relying entirely on eyesight to maneuver the bulky suits.

· 48 ·

TRUE OR FALSE: ABOUT A THIRD OF THE MASS OF THE ASTEROID BELT IS MADE UP BY ONE OBJECT.

True. Ceres is now classified as a dwarf planet, but it is almost 600 miles wide and makes up 33% of the asteroid belt's mass.

49. TRUE OR FALSE: SPACESUITS ARE SURPRISINGLY CHEAP, WITH THE MOST EXPENSIVE PART BEING THE REFLECTIVE VISOR THAT WARDS OFF RADIATION.

False on all counts. Spacesuits cost millions of dollars, with estimates ranging from $2 million to $12 million.

50. TRUE OR FALSE: MERCURY IS THE HOTTEST PLANET IN THE SOLAR SYSTEM.

False. Despite being the closest planet to the sun, Mercury is not the hottest. That honor instead goes to Venus, whose atmosphere traps heat in.

52. TRUE OR FALSE: A COMET'S TAIL IS ACTUALLY MADE UP OF MELTING ICE.

True. Comets sprout tails as they approach the sun and the heat begins to melt off some of their ice.

51. TRUE OR FALSE: NEIL ARMSTRONG CLAIMS THAT HE ACTUALLY SAID, "THAT'S ONE SMALL STEP FOR A MAN" WHEN HE LANDED ON THE MOON.

True. Audio analysis backs him up, which means we've been saying it wrong all these years.

53. TRUE OR FALSE: MARS IS RUSTY.

True! The red color of Mars comes from its oxidized soil.

54. TRUE OR FALSE: WHEN MATTER AND ANTIMATTER COME INTO CONTACT, THEY FUSE.

False. Matter and antimatter colliding would result in an enormous explosion!

55. TRUE OR FALSE: SOME OF THE MOONS IN OUR SOLAR SYSTEM HAVE MOONS OF THEIR OWN.

False. Although it is theoretically possible, the tidal forces between planet and moon tend to rip away any potential satellites.

56. TRUE OR FALSE: WE CAN STILL DETECT REMNANTS OF THE BIG BANG.

True. The echo of the big bang is still detectable in the cosmic background radiation.

• 57 •

TRUE OR FALSE: URANUS WAS ALMOST NAMED "GEORGE."

True. The astronomer who
first discovered the planet was
English, and wanted to name
it after King George as either
"George" or "Georgium." It
definitely wouldn't have fit with
the going theme...

58. **TRUE OR FALSE: MATTER MAKES UP LESS THAN 5% OF THE MASS AND ENERGY OF THE OBSERVABLE UNIVERSE.**

True. The rest is made up of dark matter and dark energy... neither of which we are even close to fully understanding.

59. **TRUE OR FALSE: SUNSPOTS ARE AREAS ON THE SURFACE OF THE SUN THAT ARE MUCH, MUCH HOTTER THAN THE REST OF THE SURFACE.**

False. It's actually the exact opposite, as sunspots can be 2,000 degrees cooler than the area around them.

60. **TRUE OR FALSE: SATURN'S RINGS ARE ALMOST AS THICK AS THE MOON.**

False. Saturn's rings are actually very thin, maxing out at just a kilometer (little more than half a mile) even at their thickest point.

61. **TRUE OR FALSE: ASTRONAUTS HAVE TO DRINK THEIR OWN PEE.**

True—mostly. Astronauts use a recycling system to capture their urine and process it back into clean drinking water.

62. TRUE OR FALSE:
WHEN SALLY RIDE
FIRST WENT TO SPACE,
NASA ASKED HER IF 100
TAMPONS WOULD BE
ENOUGH FOR HER SIX-
DAY JOURNEY.

Sadly, this is true.

63. TRUE OR FALSE: YOU CAN'T CRY IN SPACE.

True. Well, sort of: your tear ducts can still produce tears, but they don't fall. Thanks to the zero gravity environment, they just build up over your eyeballs and cloud your vision.

64. TRUE OR FALSE: BECAUSE THE SUN IS NOT SOLID, ITS TEMPERATURE IS JUST ABOUT THE SAME AT ITS CORE AS IT IS ON THE SURFACE.

False. On the surface, the sun's temperature is a toasty 10,000 degrees Fahrenheit (5,500 degrees Celsius).

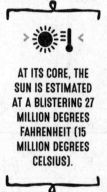

AT ITS CORE, THE SUN IS ESTIMATED AT A BLISTERING 27 MILLION DEGREES FAHRENHEIT (15 MILLION DEGREES CELSIUS).

65. TRUE OR FALSE: MILLIONS OF GALAXIES ARE MOVING AWAY FROM US TOWARD AN UNKNOWN OBJECT OUTSIDE OF OUR OBSERVABLE UNIVERSE.

True. Scientists have called this movement "Dark Flow," and we have no idea what is causing it. Some believe that they are moving toward an unseen galactic superstructure, or even something leftover from the big bang.

66. TRUE OR FALSE: ASTRONOMERS HAVE IDENTIFIED STAR SYSTEMS WITH AS MANY AS SEVEN STARS.

True. Multiple star systems are not particularly uncommon, but scientists know of two systems that contain SEVEN stars.

67. TRUE OR FALSE: MAGNETARS ARE SO MAGNETICALLY CHARGED THAT THEY COULD DISSOLVE YOUR ENTIRE MOLECULAR STRUCTURE.

Terrifyingly true. Magnetars are a particular type of neutron star, though…so it's unlikely you'll ever get close enough to one to worry.

68. TRUE OR FALSE: ALTHOUGH STARLESS "ROGUE" PLANETS ARE THEORIZED TO EXIST, THERE IS NO WAY FOR US TO DETECT THEM.

False. We have actually identified a rogue planet, inventively named CFBDSIR2149, just a hundred light-years from our solar system.

69. TRUE OR FALSE: SCIENTISTS BELIEVE THAT "DARK GALAXIES" EXIST, CONTAINING LITTLE OR NO STARS.

True. Dark galaxies would be made up almost entirely of dark matter, but we have been unable to confirm the existence of any…yet.

• 70 •

TRUE OR FALSE: AMONG
THE OBJECTS HUMANS
HAVE SENT TO SPACE
ARE PICTURES OF HUMAN
SEX ORGANS, SEA URCHIN
SPERM, A PIZZA, AND THE
REMAINS OF THE GUY WHO
DISCOVERED PLUTO.

True. Why not?

71. TRUE OR FALSE: NOVAS ARE A THING. SUPERNOVAS ARE A THING. AND HYPERNOVAS ARE A THING.

True. Just like a supernova is a supercharged version of a nova, a hypernova is a particularly violent and energetic supernova.

72. TRUE OR FALSE: GALAXIES ARE MORE OR LESS EVENLY DISTRIBUTED THROUGHOUT SPACE.

False. In fact, there are massive "galaxy filaments" that stretch across the observable universe and contain hundreds of millions of galaxies. On the other hand, there are massive voids, like the Boötes Void, where there are almost no galaxies at all for hundreds of millions of light-years.

73. TRUE OR FALSE: WE HAVE FOUND A PLANET THAT IS ALMOST AS OLD AS THE UNIVERSE ITSELF.

True. The planet, aptly nicknamed Methuselah, is estimated to have formed when the universe was less than a billion years old. Since scientists didn't believe planets could form that early in the universe's history, they were baffled.

74. TRUE OR FALSE: FOR A WHILE, SCIENTISTS THOUGHT THAT THE LARGEST OBJECT IN THE UNIVERSE WAS SOMETHING THEY HAD NAMED THE "NEWFOUND BLOB."

True. Scientists really aren't known for their inventive names…

75. **TRUE OR FALSE: ALTHOUGH THE SUN IS MASSIVE, MOST OF ITS ENERGY OUTPUT IS ABSORBED BY THE PLANETS THAT ORBIT IT.**

False. Only about one two-billionth of the energy that the sun releases hits the earth...and the other planets don't add a whole lot more to that total.

76. **TRUE OR FALSE: JUPITER IS BIGGER THAN THE REST OF THE PLANETS IN OUR SOLAR SYSTEM COMBINED.**

True.

77. **TRUE OR FALSE: URANUS ROTATES ON ITS SIDE.**

True. For some reason (probably a large impact event in its past), Uranus is tilted 90 degrees on its side. This means that its poles face the sun, and its equator is perpendicular to it!

78. **TRUE OR FALSE: THE COLDEST PLACE IN THE UNIVERSE IS ACTUALLY ON EARTH.**

True! Scientists have created an artificial environment where the temperature is just 0.000000000001 degrees Kelvin... about as close to absolute zero as we can get!

79. TRUE OR FALSE: THERE ARE STARS THAT ARE MILLIONS OF TIMES MORE LUMINOUS THAN OUR SUN.

True. The most luminous stars that we have discovered (so far) are upwards of 8-10 million times more luminous than the sun!

80. TRUE OR FALSE: THE FIRST LIVING CREATURE TO DIE IN SPACE WAS A CAT SENT TO SPACE BY NASA.

False. In fact, it was a dog sent by the Soviets, and it died when its capsule ran out of oxygen.

81. TRUE OR FALSE: SOME SCIENTISTS BELIEVE THAT WE LIVE IN A MULTIVERSE.

True! The idea that our universe is not the only universe is an idea that has gained an increasing amount of steam lately.

82. TRUE OR FALSE: WHEN GALAXIES COLLIDE, THE GRAVITATIONAL CHAOS USUALLY CAUSES ONE OR BOTH TO DISSIPATE.

False. When galaxies collide they usually come together to form a single, larger galaxy over the course of millions of years.

83. TRUE OR FALSE: THE RUSSIANS CREATED THE WORLD'S FIRST ARTIFICIAL WORMHOLE IN THE 1990S.

False. In fact, scientists still aren't completely sure whether wormholes can actually exist. So far, they are just theory.

84. TRUE OR FALSE: WE ARE STILL EXPERIENCING THE GRAVITATIONAL PULL FROM OTHER STARS THAT HAVE LONG SINCE GONE SUPERNOVA.

True. As with the sun, gravity cannot travel faster than the speed of light. Just about everything in the observable universe interacts with us in some gravitational way, and many of those stars have long since burned out.

85. TRUE OR FALSE: WE HAVE FOUND A PLANET OF BURNING ICE.

True. Gliese 436 b is burning hot, but the ice on its surface is under so much pressure that it does not evaporate.

86. TRUE OR FALSE: FOOD TASTES DIFFERENT IN SPACE.

True. Many astronauts have reported that their food preferences changed dramatically during their time in space.

• 87 •

TRUE OR FALSE: YOU CAN'T LIGHT A CANDLE IN ZERO GRAVITY.

False. Not only can you light
a candle, but also the flame it
produces will be round and blue.

88. TRUE OR FALSE: THE GRAVITY OF THE LOCAL GROUP (OUR GROUP OF GALAXIES) WILL KEEP THE MILKY WAY FROM COLLIDING WITH ANY OF ITS OTHER GALAXIES.

False. In a few hundred million years, the Milky Way will collide with the Andromeda Galaxy.

89. TRUE OR FALSE: EARLY ASTRONAUT TOILETS WERE SO BAD THAT FECES SOMETIMES FLOATED THROUGH THE SPACE CAPSULE.

True. Read the transcript of the Apollo 10 mission sometime. Thank me later.

90. TRUE OR FALSE: RICHARD NIXON HAD A SPEECH PREPARED JUST IN CASE NEIL ARMSTRONG AND BUZZ ALDRIN DIED ON THE MOON.

True. The speech has been declassified and can now be read online.

STAR-STUDDED
Pop Culture Facts

Movies. TV shows. Celebrities. These things captivate us, distract us, and excite us. They can be great, they can be terrible, and they can be fascinating. They can also be downright unbelievable!

You could fill a book with weird facts about any one aspect of pop culture, but here we'll just focus on the weirdest, wildest, and most outrageous of them all. Although these facts sound like bullshit, you can rest assured that they are completely true.

1. IN *STAR WARS*, DARTH VADER NEVER SAYS "LUKE, I AM YOUR FATHER."

Similarly, the famous quote "play it again, Sam," is never actually uttered in *Casablanca*, and the witch in *Snow White* never says "mirror, mirror, on the wall"—she says "magic mirror."

2. ARNOLD SCHWARZENEGGER ALMOST MISSED OUT ON THE TITLE ROLE IN *TERMINATOR* TO NONE OTHER THAN O.J. SIMPSON.

Simpson would eventually be passed over in part because he was viewed as too "likable" and "innocent."

3. FAMOUS VIDEO GAME AND MOVIE LOCATION SILENT HILL IS BASED ON AN ACTUAL TOWN.

The ghost town of Centralia, Pennsylvania is located over an abandoned mine where a coal fire has been raging for decades.

4. EVEN THOUGH EVERYONE KNOWS WHAT THE FUZZY LITTLE BEARS ARE CALLED, THE WORD "EWOK" NEVER APPEARS IN *THE RETURN OF THE JEDI*.

5. ALTHOUGH SEAN CONNERY PLAYED HARRISON FORD'S FATHER IN *INDIANA JONES AND THE LAST CRUSADE*, CONNERY IS JUST 12 YEARS OLDER THAN FORD.

6. MORE TICKETS WERE SOLD TO SEE *GONE WITH THE WIND* IN THEATERS THAN PEOPLE LIVING IN AMERICA AT ITS RELEASE.

In 1939, America's population was just 130 million. Over 200 million tickets have been sold during *Gone with the Wind*'s theatrical runs.

7. AMONG THE ACTORS WHO AUDITIONED FOR HAN SOLO IN THE ORIGINAL *STAR WARS* WERE KURT RUSSELL, ROBERT ENGLUND, AND EVEN SYLVESTER STALLONE.

8. DAVID PROWSE, WHO PLAYED DARTH VADER IN THE ORIGINAL *STAR WARS* TRILOGY, WAS INITIALLY UNAWARE THAT HIS VOICE WOULD NOT BE USED FOR THE CHARACTER.

According to the actor, dialogue coming from under the mask was unusable and needed to be dubbed over in post-production. George Lucas and the rest of the production team made the financial decision to use local actor James Earl Jones rather than fly Prowse over to America to re-record a handful of lines.

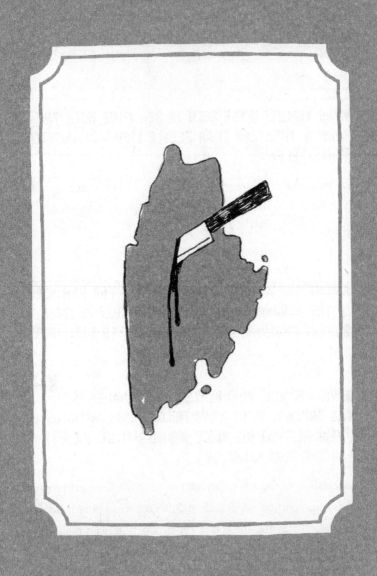

· 9 ·

MAINE IS A REALLY POPULAR STATE FOR FICTIONAL MURDERS.

Maybe it's just because of its remote location, but Maine has been used as the setting for a surprising number of fictional mysteries and thrillers. Notably, the fictional towns of Derry, created by Stephen King and used in many of his works, and Cabot Cove, the setting of *Murder, She Wrote*, remain in the public eye today.

10. MUSICIAN JOHN CAGE PRODUCED A MUSICAL PIECE, APTLY TITLED *AS SLOW AS POSSIBLE*, THAT IS DESIGNED TO BE PLAYED OVER 639 YEARS.

A performance is currently underway in Halberstadt, Germany, using an organ specifically designed for the performance. It began in 2001 and will not conclude until 2640.

11. ACCORDING TO LEGEND, HARD ROCKING BAND ALICE COOPER CHOSE THEIR NAME AFTER USING AN OUIJA BOARD TO COMMUNICATE WITH A SPIRIT NAMED ALICE COOPER.

The band has disputed this over the years, but the rumor appears to originate with frontman Vincent Furnier himself.

12. MARTIN SHEEN'S REAL NAME IS RAMÓN ANTONIO GERARDO ESTÉVEZ.

His son, Emilio Estévez, also went on to become an actor. One of his other sons, Carlos Estévez, is also an actor—better known as Charlie Sheen.

13. CHARLIE CHAPLIN ONCE ENTERED A CHARLIE CHAPLIN LOOK-ALIKE CONTEST—AND LOST.

It is hard to be 100 percent certain that this happened—after all, official records of a Charlie Chaplin look-alike contest are unlikely to exist—but even the Association Chaplin, the historical society dedicated to Chaplin, allows that it "may be true."

14. IN 1929, FAMOUS TELEVISION DOG RIN TIN TIN RECEIVED THE MOST VOTES FOR THE ACADEMY AWARD FOR BEST ACTOR.

Sadly, he did not win the award. The Academy was concerned that if they gave the first ever Best Actor award to a dog, the awards would never be taken seriously.

15. THOUGH THEY LOOK EXACTLY ALIKE, MARY KATE AND ASHLEY OLSEN ARE FRATERNAL TWINS, NOT IDENTICAL TWINS.

• 16 •

THE BEATLES BREAKUP HAPPENED AT DISNEY WORLD.

John Lennon signed the paperwork formalizing the band's split while staying at a Disney World hotel.

17. YODA FROM *STAR WARS*, COOKIE MONSTER FROM *SESAME STREET*, AND MISS PIGGY FROM *THE MUPPET SHOW* WERE ALL VOICED BY THE SAME PERSON.

Frank Oz is one of the world's most prolific voice actors. Other characters in his repertoire include Fozzie Bear, Sam the Eagle, and Animal.

18. *THE ALPHABET SONG* AND *TWINKLE, TWINKLE, LITTLE STAR* HAVE THE SAME TUNE.

19. FRANK SINATRA STARRED IN A PREQUEL TO *DIE HARD*.

Die Hard was based on a book by Roderick Thorp, and was a sequel to his earlier work, *The Detective*, which was optioned into a movie starring Frank Sinatra. Rumor has it that Frank Sinatra even had right of first refusal for the leading role in *Die Hard*. Since Sinatra was 73 when *Die Hard* was filmed, he thankfully recused himself.

20. WOODY IN *TOY STORY* HAS A LAST NAME.

It wasn't revealed until 2009, but Woody's official last name is "Pride."

21. IN THE MOVIE *HOME ALONE*, THE PICTURE OF BUZZ'S GIRLFRIEND THAT KEVIN FINDS IS ACTUALLY A BOY IN A WIG.

The director thought it would be mean to use a picture of an actual girl as an "ugly" gag, and wisely decided to go a different route.

22. THE EFFECTS USED TO RECREATE MISSILE LAUNCHES IN *TOP GUN* WERE SO REALISTIC THAT THE NAVY LAUNCHED AN INVESTIGATION TO DETERMINE WHETHER REAL MISSILES HAD ACTUALLY BEEN LAUNCHED.

The Navy actually authorized the use of two missiles, but the recreations put together by the movie's effects team were realistic enough to cause suspicion that more than the allotted two had been launched!

· 23 ·

THE LEADING ROLE IN *FORREST GUMP* WAS ORIGINALLY OFFERED TO JOHN TRAVOLTA.

24. LEONARDO DICAPRIO DIDN'T DRAW THE SKETCH OF KATE WINSLET IN *TITANIC*...BUT DIRECTOR JAMES CAMERON DID.

25. THE MASK THAT MICHAEL MYERS WEARS IN *HALLOWEEN* WAS ACTUALLY A WHITE CAPTAIN KIRK MASK.

26. ACTOR DOLPH LUNDGREN (BEST KNOWN FOR PLAYING IVAN DRAGO IN *ROCKY IV*) HOLDS A MASTER'S DEGREE IN CHEMICAL ENGINEERING.

27. OVER THE COURSE OF HIS CAREER, ACTOR CHRISTOPHER LEE PLAYED VILLAINS IN SEVERAL OF THE MOST SUCCESSFUL FRANCHISES OF ALL TIME, INCLUDING *THE LORD OF THE RINGS*, *JAMES BOND*, *STAR WARS*, AND *DRACULA*.

All told, Lee was one of the best villainous actors of all-time... though in real life he was said to be a very nice guy!

28. HAROLD RAMIS ORIGINALLY WANTED PINK FLOYD TO RECORD THE SOUNDTRACK FOR *CADDYSHACK*.

Sadly (or maybe fortunately?), the band declined the offer.

29. IN THE POST-APOCALYPTIC CLASSIC *THE ROAD WARRIOR*, MEL GIBSON'S LEAD CHARACTER (MAD MAX) HAS JUST 16 LINES OF DIALOGUE.

30. IN THE *STAR WARS* TRILOGY, GEORGE LUCAS' ORIGINAL NAME FOR YODA WAS "BUFFY."

The character's full name was to be "Bunden Debannen"— Buffy for short. Even after settling on "Yoda," the character originally had a first name: Minch.

31. IN BLACK AND WHITE FILMS, CHOCOLATE SYRUP WAS OFTEN USED IN PLACE OF FAKE BLOOD.

Fake blood often didn't seem dark enough on camera, so directors were forced to get creative. For instance, that iconic shower scene in *Psycho*? It's chocolate syrup you see.

DARK CHOCOLATE 70% COCOA

• 32 •

LED ZEPPELIN WROTE MULTIPLE SONGS ABOUT *THE LORD OF THE RINGS*.

"Ramble On," "The Battle of Evermore," and "Misty Mountain Hop" all contain clear references to the famous novel. Many people speculate that other songs contain more subtle references, too.

33. PAUL MCCARTNEY ONCE RELEASED AN ALBUM UNDER THE NAME THRILLS THRILLINGTON.

Percy "Thrills" Thrillington, to be exact. The title of the album? *Thrillington*, of course.

34. FORMER BEATLES DRUMMER RINGO STARR WAS THE ORIGINAL NARRATOR OF THE CHILDREN'S TELEVISION SHOW *THOMAS THE TANK ENGINE*.

35. DURING HIS PERFORMANCES IN *JAMES BOND*, SEAN CONNERY ALWAYS WORE A WIG.

This should come as no surprise to those who know Connery primarily from his later work—the actor is famously bald.

36. GENE RODDENBERRY ORIGINALLY WANTED PATRICK STEWART TO WEAR A WIG FOR HIS ICONIC *STAR TREK* ROLE AS CAPTAIN JEAN-LUC PICARD.

Later, when a reporter noted that they would surely have a cure for baldness by the 24th century, Roddenberry is said to have responded, "No, by the 24th century no one will care."

37. ELVIS PRESLEY NEVER WROTE ANY
OF HIS OWN SONGS.

A GIANT SHIELD
BUG'S MARKINGS
ONCE RESEMBLED
THE KING'S HAIRDO

38. THE FAMOUS "WILHELM SCREAM"
HAS BEEN USED
IN HUNDREDS OF MOVIES
AND TELEVISION SHOWS
OVER THE YEARS.

The scream has become an in-joke among moviemakers.
Originally from the 1951 movie *Distant Drums*, the sound
effect has been used onscreen in everything from *Star Wars*
and *Star Trek* to *Toy Story* and *Lethal Weapon*.

39. ONE OF THE BIGGEST BOX OFFICE BOMBS IN HISTORY,
JOHN CARTER LOST AN ESTIMATED $200 MILLION
DOLLARS FOR ITS PRODUCTION COMPANY.

The sad thing is, it was actually a pretty decent movie!

40. SEAN CONNERY TURNED DOWN THE ROLE OF GANDALF
IN *THE LORD OF THE RINGS* BECAUSE HE DIDN'T
UNDERSTAND THE SCRIPT.

When the franchise was wildly successful, he reevaluated his
thinking…only to accept a role in box office bomb *The League
of Extraordinary Gentlemen*.

· 41 ·

IN *THE WIZARD OF OZ*, THE DOG PLAYING TOTO WAS PAID AN ACTUAL SALARY.

He was paid $125 a week! This was more than many of the film's human actors were paid.

42. THE ICONIC SCENE IN *RAIDERS OF THE LOST ARK* WHERE INDIANA JONES SHOOTS THE SWORDSMAN WAS NEVER SUPPOSED TO HAPPEN.

It turns out Harrison Ford was too sick to perform the scene as scripted...so the production team improvised.

43. KEVIN SMITH'S ICONIC MOVIE *CLERKS* WAS FILMED ON A BUDGET OF LESS THAN $28,000.

Clerks was filmed on just $27,575, although post-production expenses after filming was complete pushed the total to about $230,000—still an impressively low budget!

44. FAMOUS PORNOGRAPHIC ACTOR RON JEREMY HAS HAD MINOR ROLES (OR CAMEOS) IN MANY NON-PORNOGRAPHIC MOVIES.

His appearances include *The Boondock Saints*, *Ghostbusters*, and *Crank: High Voltage*.

45. THE PRODUCERS OF *MEET THE FOCKERS* HAD TO FIND ACTUAL FOCKERS.

The MPAA wouldn't allow the title of the film to stand unless they could prove that "Focker" was an actual last name.

46. TRUE OR FALSE: THE INJURIES ON LUKE SKYWALKER'S FACE WHEN HE IS ATTACKED BY THE SNOW MONSTER IN *THE EMPIRE STRIKES BACK* WERE REAL.

True. Actor Mark Hamill had gotten into a car accident and severely injured his face. Rather than delay filming, George Lucas simply worked it into the script.

47. TRUE OR FALSE: IN THE MOVIE *MEAN GIRLS*, AMY POEHLER PLAYS RACHEL MCADAMS' MOTHER DESPITE THE FACT THAT SHE IS ACTUALLY YOUNGER THAN RACHEL MCADAMS.

False. But the difference isn't that great…Poehler is just seven years older than McAdams.

48. TRUE OR FALSE: INDIA'S BOLLYWOOD MOVIE INDUSTRY PRODUCES MORE MOVIES EACH YEAR THAN HOLLYWOOD.

True. Bollywood produces upwards of 1,000 movies per year—although they typically receive less acclaim than their Hollywood counterparts.

49. TRUE OR FALSE: 2006'S *CASINO ROYALE* WAS THE FIRST BOND MOVIE THAT COULD BE WATCHED IN CHINA.

True. It was the first film in the *James Bond* series that the Chinese censor board approved.

50. TRUE OR FALSE: THE FIRST INTERRACIAL KISS IN TELEVISION HISTORY HAPPENED ON *STAR TREK*.

True. Although the network originally didn't want to air it, William Shatner reportedly sabotaged all of the other shoots, forcing the network to run the kiss.

51. TRUE OR FALSE: THE FIRST TELEVISION COMMERCIAL EVER WAS A CAR COMMERCIAL.

False. It was actually a commercial for watches, and it aired in 1941.

52. TRUE OR FALSE: ACTOR JIM CAVIEZEL WAS STRUCK BY LIGHTNING WHILE PORTRAYING JESUS IN *THE PASSION OF THE CHRIST*.

True. Caviezel suffered a large number of calamities during the filming, but this one seemed like a bit of an omen.

53. TRUE OR FALSE: BRYAN ADAMS' FAMOUS SONG "SUMMER OF '69" IS NAMED AFTER THE SEX POSITION, NOT THE YEAR.

True. In fact, Adams was just 9 years old during the summer of 1969.

54. TRUE OR FALSE: THE ROLLING STONES PERFORMED IN *BACK TO THE FUTURE 3*.

False. But ZZ Top did!

55. TRUE OR FALSE: THE WORD "FUCK" WAS ONCE SAID OVER 1,000 TIMES IN ONE MOVIE.

False. But *Swearnet: The Movie* came close with the word appearing 935 times—a record amount!

56. TRUE OR FALSE: *BATTLEFIELD EARTH* WAS WRITTEN BY THE FOUNDER OF SCIENTOLOGY.

True. L. Ron Hubbard was a well-known science fiction writer in addition to being the founder of Scientology.

• 57 •

TRUE OR FALSE: IF YOU PLAY "STAIRWAY TO HEAVEN" BACKWARDS, YOU CAN HEAR SATANIC MESSAGES.

True…sort of. If you listen closely, it definitely sounds like there are some weird messages in there. But it would have been almost impossible for the band to do intentionally, and they have long denied it.

58. TRUE OR FALSE: IN THE FIRST *STAR WARS* FILM, DARTH VADER HAS JUST OVER 10 MINUTES OF SCREEN TIME.

True. Vader cemented himself as an iconic villain despite appearing onscreen for only 12 minutes.

59. TRUE OR FALSE: THE CARPET IN SID'S HOUSE IN TOY STORY IS BASED ON THE CARPET FROM ALFRED HITCHCOCK'S *PSYCHO*.

False...but it IS based on the carpet from *The Shining*.

60. TRUE OR FALSE: NO ONE HAS EVER GUESSED THE EXACT PRICE OF THEIR SHOWCASE ON *THE PRICE IS RIGHT*.

False. It has happened exactly once in the show's history... and, of course, everyone accused him of cheating. By all accounts, it appears to have been legitimate.

61. TRUE OR FALSE: NICOLAS CAGE IS NAMED AFTER COMIC BOOK HERO LUKE CAGE.

True. "Nicolas Cage" is just a stage name (his real name is Nicolas Coppola), and he chose it based on the famed comic book character.

62. TRUE OR FALSE: THE MAXIMUM AMOUNT THAT A CONTESTANT CAN WIN ON *JEOPARDY* IS $566,400.

True. In the unlikely event that a contestant answered every question correctly, got Daily Doubles on the final questions of each round and wagered everything each time, then answered Final Jeopardy correctly and again bet everything…they would wind up with $566,400. Of course, this has never (and probably will never) happen.

63. TRUE OR FALSE: OUR REAL-LIFE PLANET EARTH EXISTS IN MARVEL COMICS UNDER THE NAME LEE-PRIME (AFTER CREATOR STAN LEE).

False. Our Earth does exist, but it is under the designation Earth-1218 (or Earth-Prime).

64. TRUE OR FALSE: DC COMICS BOASTS A SUPERHERO NAMED ARMS-FALL-OFF-BOY.

Somehow, this is true. Arms-Fall-Off-Boy predictably has the power to detach his own limbs and use them as weapons. Equally predictably, he has not made many appearances.

• 65 •

TRUE OR FALSE: THE FICTIONAL CITY OF METROPOLIS (THE HOME OF SUPERMAN) IS LOCATED IN NEW YORK.

False. Believe it or not, Metropolis is canonically located in Delaware!

66. TRUE OR FALSE: STEVEN SPIELBERG SUBMITTED *SCHINDLER'S LIST* AS HIS FINAL PROJECT FOR FILM SCHOOL.

True. Spielberg decided to go back and finish film school in 2002, and somewhat cheekily submitted the well-known film as his final project.

67. TRUE OR FALSE: OPRAH WINFREY'S REAL NAME IS SUSANNAH GAIL WINFREY.

False. But interestingly, Oprah isn't her real name either. It's Orpah, after a biblical figure. People simply mispronounced her name so often that she stuck with it!

68. TRUE OR FALSE: SPOCK ONCE BEAT WOLVERINE IN A FIGHT.

True. In a Marvel Comics / *Star Trek* crossover, Spock calmly defeated Wolverine with his trademark nerve pinch.

69. TRUE OR FALSE: MATTHEW FOX'S CHARACTER IN *LOST*, JACK, WAS ORIGINALLY SUPPOSED TO DIE IN THE VERY FIRST EPISODE.

True. Thankfully, the showrunners liked Fox enough to keep Jack around, as he would become the main character in the show.

70. TRUE OR FALSE: LILY ALLEN'S SONG "ALFIE" IS ABOUT THE ACTOR WHO PLAYS THEON GREYJOY IN *GAME OF THRONES*.

True. Theon is played by Alfie Allen…Lily's brother!

71. TRUE OR FALSE: KEANU REEVES WAS OFFERED THE LEAD ROLE IN *WILD WILD WEST* BUT TURNED IT DOWN TO STAR IN *THE MATRIX*.

False. Actually, it was Will Smith who turned down the lead role in *The Matrix* to star in legendary flop *Wild Wild West*.

72. TRUE OR FALSE: KELSEY GRAMMER ONCE PLAYED A CAPTAIN ON *STAR TREK*.

True. Grammer appeared in the episode "Cause and Effect" on *Star Trek: The Next Generation*.

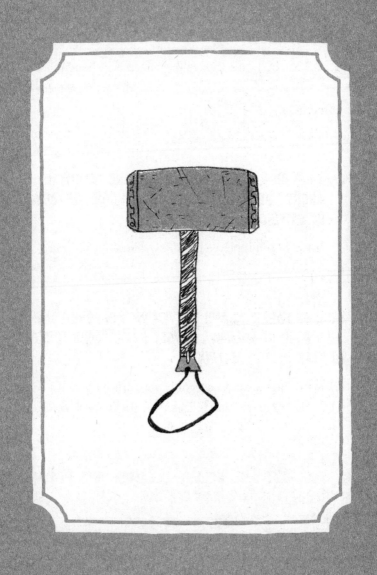

TRUE OR FALSE: OVER TWO DOZEN PEOPLE HAVE WIELDED THOR'S HAMMER IN VARIOUS CONTINUITIES.

True. Although Thor's hammer is famously specific to him, more characters than you might think have wielded it over the years.

74. TRUE OR FALSE: *THE ADDAMS FAMILY* SET WAS ENTIRELY BLACK AND WHITE TO KEEP THE ACTORS IN CHARACTER.

False. The set was actually pink—quite a departure from the show's playfully dark theme!

75. TRUE OR FALSE: DESPITE BEING A COMMON JOKE TODAY, ROBIN NEVER ACTUALLY SAYS "HOLY _____, BATMAN!" DURING ANY *BATMAN* EPISODES.

False. The phrase is actually uttered (with various words inserted) over 300 times!

76. TRUE OR FALSE: THE ICONIC THEME SONG OF *THE X-FILES* WAS CREATED BY ACCIDENT.

True. One of the producers accidentally hit the "echo" button on the control pad, and they liked it so much they kept it.

77. TRUE OR FALSE: KRAMER'S FIRST NAME IN *SEINFELD* IS "COSMO."

True.

78. TRUE OR FALSE: THE *STAR TREK* TRANSPORTER WAS "INVENTED" BY A PRODUCTION ASSISTANT WHO WONDERED WHY THE FUTURE WOULDN'T HAVE TELEPORTATION.

False. It was actually invented as a cost-saving idea to prevent having to film the *Enterprise* taking off and landing all the time!

79. TRUE OR FALSE: JOHN WAYNE WAS OFFERED A LEAD ROLE IN *BLAZING SADDLES*.

True. Sadly, The Duke turned it down, but made a point to tell Mel Brooks how excited he was to see it.

80. TRUE OR FALSE: *CURB YOUR ENTHUSIASM* GOT A MAN CONVICTED OF MURDER.

False. Just the opposite, in fact! When an accused murderer could be seen in the background shot during an episode, his alibi was verified and he was freed from prison.

81. TRUE OR FALSE: GEORGE STEINBRENNER ABSOLUTELY HATED HIS COMEDIC PORTRAYAL ON *SEINFELD*.

False. Actually, Steinbrenner quickly came to love both the series and his humorous role.

• 82 •

TRUE OR FALSE: BRAD PITT'S FIRST ACTING GIG WAS DRESSING UP AS A GIANT CHICKEN.

True. Pitt wore a chicken costume
for his job at El Pollo Loco.

83. TRUE OR FALSE: JAMES EARL JONES WAS OFFERED THE LEAD ROLE IN *STAR TREK: DEEP SPACE NINE*.

True. The role eventually went to Avery Brooks.

84. TRUE OR FALSE: IN *JUDGE DREDD*, SYLVESTER STALLONE INSISTED ON STAYING TRUE TO THE COMICS AND KEEPING HIS HELMET ON THE ENTIRE TIME.

IN 2012'S *DREDD*, KARL URBAN CHOSE A MORE TRADITIONAL TAKE ON THE CHARACTER AND NEVER REMOVED THE HELMET.

False. Stallone couldn't wait to take the helmet off, and spent most of the movie not wearing it.

85. TRUE OR FALSE: HELEN MIRREN IS DESCENDED FROM A WOMAN WHO WAS ACCUSED OF WITCHCRAFT DURING THE FAMOUS SALEM WITCH TRIALS.

False. It's actually Sarah Jessica Parker who can trace her lineage back to this unfortunate ancestor!

86. TRUE OR FALSE: FAMOUS CHILDREN'S BOOK *GREEN EGGS AND HAM* CONTAINS JUST 50 DIFFERENT WORDS.

True. Dr. Seuss made a bet with a colleague that he could write a successful book using just 50 words—and he won!

87. TRUE OR FALSE: ACTOR TIM ALLEN ALMOST WENT TO PRISON FOR LIFE BEFORE BECOMING A FAMOUS ACTOR.

True. The *Home Improvement* star was a drug dealer before he became an actor, and avoided significant prison time by giving up the names of other dealers.

88. TRUE OR FALSE: STEVE BUSCEMI RETURNED TO HIS FORMER JOB AS A FIREFIGHTER AFTER THE 9/11 ATTACKS.

True. Buscemi worked 12-hour shifts to help rescue people from the rubble after the attacks. Before becoming an actor, he had been a New York City firefighter.

89. TRUE OR FALSE: WOODY HARRELSON'S FATHER WAS A SECRET SERVICE AGENT WHO NEARLY PREVENTED THE DEATH OF PRESIDENT JOHN F. KENNEDY.

False. Actually, Harrelson's father was an assassin who murdered a federal judge and claimed to have had a hand in the Kennedy assassination (this last claim is widely discredited).

90. TRUE OR FALSE: SAMUEL L. JACKSON ONCE HELD MARTIN LUTHER KING, SR. HOSTAGE.

True. During his college days, Jackson was part of a group of students that held the Morehead College Board of Trustees hostage. Among the hostages was Martin Luther King, Sr.

[OUTRAGEOUS FACTS
FROM THE
World of Sports]

Athletes are amazing. They perform outrageous feats of strength and agility that you and I can only dream of. Most of them have dedicated their lives to being as good at their craft as they can possibly be—and it shows. Whether it's Barry Bonds slugging hundreds of home runs or Wayne Gretzky scoring a truly incredible amount of goals, athletes live to dazzle and amaze us.

In fact, athletes wow us with new records and amazing performances so often that sometimes we become numb to it. A 500-foot home run? Yawn. A touchdown pass that deflected off three different people? Ho hum. It's almost sad how ordinary the extraordinary has become to us.

Well, no longer! Here you'll find some of the most incredible sports facts in history. If you've forgotten what it's like to be surprised by incredible sporting accomplishments, prepare to have your mind blown.

1. IF WAYNE GRETZKY NEVER TOOK A SINGLE SHOT IN THE NHL, HE WOULD STILL BE THE LEAGUE'S ALL-TIME POINTS LEADER.

Gretzky retired with 2,857 points (goals + assists), 970 more than the next closest player. Even if you took away all 894 of Gretzky's career goals, he would still have more points than anyone in history.

2. HALL OF FAME BASKETBALL PLAYER SHAQUILLE O'NEAL MADE JUST ONE THREE-POINT SHOT IN HIS ENTIRE CAREER.

He only ever attempted 22 three-pointers, giving him a dismal 4.5% career three-point shooting percentage.

3. "MIXED PAINTING" WAS ONCE AN OLYMPIC EVENT.

At various points in history, the Olympics have included competitions in categories including painting, engraving, architecture, literature, and town planning.

4. WILT CHAMBERLAIN ONCE AVERAGED OVER 50 POINTS PER GAME FOR AN ENTIRE SEASON.

The next best season scoring average is almost 12 points fewer.

THE STANLEY CUP HAS SEVERAL TYPOS ENGRAVED ON IT.

The most egregious are probably
"BOSTON BRUINS" being spelled
as "BQSTQN BRUINS" and
"TORONTO MAPLE LEAFS"
being spelled "TORONTO MAPLE
LEAES," but a surprising number of
players' names have been misspelled
over the years.

6. THE OLYMPICS HAVE BEEN HOSTED BY MULTIPLE COUNTRIES THAT NO LONGER EXIST.

West Germany, Yugoslavia, and the USSR have all hosted the games in the past.

7. MARTIN BRODEUR IS THE ALL-TIME LEADING SCORER AMONG NHL GOALIES. HE SCORED THREE GOALS.

His first goal came in 1997, and his last came in 2013. Only one other goalie (Ron Hextall) has scored more than one goal.

8. THE MOTHER OF FORMER NBA STAR GRANT HILL WAS HILLARY CLINTON'S ROOMMATE AT WELLESLEY.

9. JACKIE MITCHELL, ONE OF THE FIRST (AND ONLY) FEMALE PLAYERS IN THE MAJOR LEAGUE BASEBALL SYSTEM, ONCE STRUCK OUT BABE RUTH AND LOU GEHRIG IN CONSECUTIVE AT-BATS.

The strikeouts occurred during a minor league exhibition game against the Yankees. While there is some debate about whether the strikeouts were part of a publicity stunt, Babe Ruth's reported anger and frustration after being struck out indicate that they were legitimate.

10. BEFORE BABE RUTH, MLB'S CAREER HOME RUN RECORD WAS JUST 138.

When the Babe retired, the new record was 714.

11. THE DENVER BRONCOS HAVE REACHED THE SUPER BOWL 8 TIMES, BUT NOT ONCE HAVE THEY STARTED A QUARTERBACK THAT THEY DRAFTED.

Craig Morton (1), John Elway (5), and Peyton Manning (2) have all started Super Bowls for the Broncos. All three were drafted by other teams and later acquired by the Broncos.

12. AT ONE TIME, THE USA ROCK PAPER SCISSORS LEAGUE WAS A REAL THING.

It even featured a $50,000 prize for its champion!

13. THERE IS A MINOR LEAGUE BASEBALL TEAM CALLED THE MONTGOMERY BISCUITS.

They play in Montgomery, Alabama, and their logo features a biscuit with googly eyes and a pat of butter for a tongue.

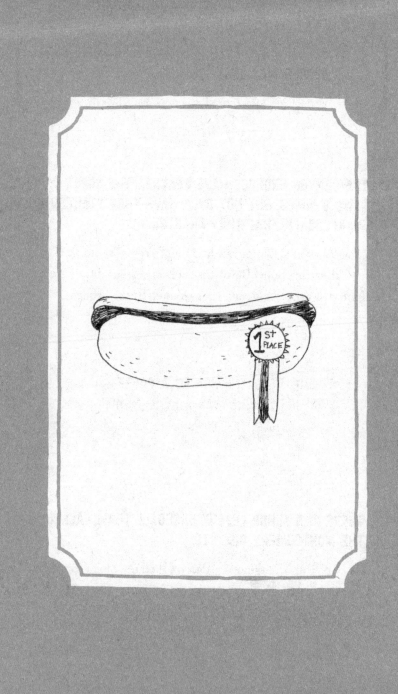

· 14 ·

THE WORLD'S BEST COMPETITIVE EATERS CAN EAT AN AVERAGE OF ONE HOT DOG EVERY 8.5 SECONDS.

In 2016, Joey Chestnut ate a record 70 hot dogs in just 10 minutes, cementing his place at the top of the competitive eating world.

15. "CHESS BOXING" IS A REAL SPORT, AND IT'S EXACTLY WHAT IT SOUNDS LIKE.

For hundreds of years, people cried out "why can't we combine chess and boxing?" And lo! In 1992, they did.

16. NEW YORK METS PITCHER DOCK ELLIS ONCE PITCHED A NO-HITTER WHILE REPORTEDLY HIGH ON LSD.

17. A WOK ISN'T JUST A COOKING IMPLEMENT. IT CAN ALSO BE A SLED.

That's according to the participants in the Wok World Championship, anyway. Teams of racers use modified woks in one- and four-person "woksleds" to travel down bobsled tracks.

18. A GERMAN NAMED JOE ALEXANDER ONCE BROKE 24 CONCRETE BLOCKS WHILE HOLDING AN EGG IN HIS SMASHIN' HAND.

19. NOLAN RYAN HAD SEVEN NO-HITTERS IN HIS MLB CAREER, BUT NO PERFECT GAMES.

This is probably because Nolan Ryan is the MLB career leader in batters walked. His 2,795 career walks are almost 1,000 more than the next closest pitcher!

20. DURING THE 1903 MLB SEASON, PITCHER ED DOHENY WON 16 GAMES...AND WAS COMMITTED TO AN ASYLUM FOR THE "CRIMINALLY INSANE."

Sadly, Doheny would spend the rest of his life in the asylum.

21. FOR 43 YEARS, THE NFL RECORD FOR THE LONGEST MADE FIELD GOAL WAS HELD BY A MAN WITH NO TOES ON HIS KICKING FOOT.

Tom Dempsey was born with neither toes on his right foot nor fingers on his right hand, but his 63-yard field goal in 1970 wasn't matched until 1998. It wasn't broken until 2013!

22. IN 1993, YANKEES PITCHER JIM ABBOTT THREW A NO-HITTER DESPITE BEING BORN WITHOUT A RIGHT HAND.

The hard-throwing lefty didn't let his missing hand stop him, and enjoyed a decade-long career in the major leagues.

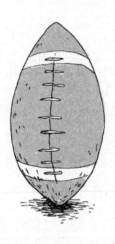

23. NO NFL GAME HAS
EVER BEEN FORFEITED.

24. THE NFL, NBA, AND MLB HAVE ALL HAD ONE PLAYER WIN THE CHAMPIONSHIP MVP WHILE PLAYING FOR THE LOSING TEAM.

Dallas Cowboys linebacker Chuck Howley won MVP of Super Bowl V, Los Angeles Lakers guard Jerry West won the NBA Finals MVP in 1969, and New York Yankees baseman Bobby Richardson won the World Series MVP in 1960. Although the NHL does not have a "finals MVP" award, four goalies have won the Conn Smythe Trophy for best overall playoff performance despite playing for the Stanley Cup-losing team.

25. IN THE HISTORY OF THE NFL, ONLY ONE LEFT-HANDED QUARTERBACK HAS MADE IT INTO THE HALL OF FAME: STEVE YOUNG.

26. JACKIE ROBINSON WAS NOT THE FIRST BLACK PLAYER IN MAJOR LEAGUE BASEBALL.

William Edward White, a former slave, served as a one-game replacement player in 1879. Moses Fleetwood Walker lasted slightly longer, playing nearly a full season in 1884, 63 years before Jackie Robinson made his historic debut.

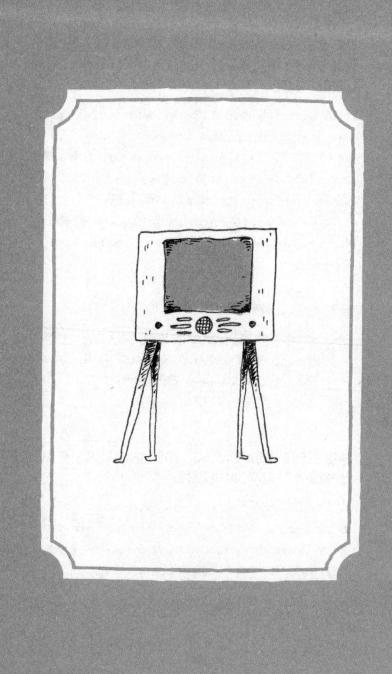

• 27 •

**ONLY ABOUT 1,000
PEOPLE WATCHED
THE FIRST TELEVISED
FOOTBALL GAME.**

In 1939, not a lot of people
had televisions!

28. HALL OF FAME MLB PITCHER HOYT WILHELM HIT A HOME RUN IN HIS VERY FIRST MAJOR LEAGUE AT-BAT. HE NEVER HIT ANOTHER HOME RUN OVER THE REMAINDER OF HIS CAREER OF 21 YEARS.

29. PETE ROSE WAS BANNED FROM BASEBALL BY PAUL GIAMATTI'S DAD.

The MLB commissioner during the Pete Rose gambling scandal was A. Bartlett Giamatti, and it was he who brought down the hammer on Rose.

30. BILL BUCKNER HAS MORE CAREER HITS THAN TED WILLIAMS.

Of course, that's not what Red Sox fans remember him for.

31. BETWEEN 1982 AND 1998, CAL RIPKEN, JR. DID NOT MISS A SINGLE BALTIMORE ORIOLES GAME.

His record of 2,632 consecutive games played still stands today, and will almost certainly never be broken.

32. THE ONLY TEAM TO SCORE THREE TOUCHDOWNS IN UNDER ONE MINUTE IN THE NFL IS THE NEW ENGLAND PATRIOTS. AND THEY'VE DONE IT TWICE.

You may remember the second time, as it involved the infamous Mark Sanchez "butt fumble," which was returned for a touchdown.

33. WALTER PAYTON ONCE THREW A TOUCHDOWN PASS, CAUGHT A TOUCHDOWN PASS, AND RAN FOR A TOUCHDOWN IN THE SAME GAME.

Only one other player has ever accomplished that feat (David Patten of the New England Patriots).

34. DURING WWII, SO MANY NFL PLAYERS WERE FIGHTING IN THE WAR THAT THE RIVAL PHILADELPHIA EAGLES AND PITTSBURGH STEELERS TEMPORARILY TEAMED UP TO FORM THE "STEAGLES."

35. BRAD JOHNSON, THEN THE QUARTERBACK OF THE MINNESOTA VIKINGS, ONCE THREW A TOUCHDOWN PASS TO HIMSELF.

The pass was batted at the line of scrimmage and came straight back to Johnson, who caught it and ran it into the end zone. This is the only time in NFL history that a player has thrown a touchdown pass to himself.

36. SWEDISH SOCCER PLAYER STEFAN SCHWARZ HAD A CLAUSE IN HIS CONTRACT THAT FORBADE HIM FROM TRAVELING TO SPACE.

37. BILL SHARMAN HAS THE HONOR OF BEING THE ONLY PLAYER TO BE EJECTED FROM AN MLB GAME WITHOUT EVER ACTUALLY APPEARING IN ONE.

Sharman was called up to the Dodgers and was ejected along with the rest of the team's bench after what the team viewed as a bad call by the umpire. Don't worry though…he went on to be a Hall of Fame *basketball* player for the Boston Celtics.

38. LEGEND HAS IT THAT HALL OF FAME BASEBALL PLAYER WADE BOGGS ONCE DRANK 107 BEERS IN ONE DAY WHILE TRAVELING WITH THE TEAM.

39. NOT TO BE OUTDONE, WRESTLER ANDRE THE GIANT ONCE CLAIMED TO HAVE CONSUMED 119 BEERS IN ONE SITTING...AND A FRIEND ALLEGES HE ONCE SAW HIM DRINK 156.

40. NFL SAFETY RONNIE LOTT ONCE HAD A FINGER AMPUTATED DURING A GAME.

Lott broke his pinky finger and wanted to avoid leaving the game—not to mention the long recovery time associated with the break. Rather than go through that, he had the doctor cut it off.

41. THE VERY FIRST PICK IN THE VERY FIRST NFL DRAFT NEVER PLAYED A SINGLE GAME IN THE LEAGUE.

Jay Berwanger never signed with a team, due to salary concerns and a desire to compete in the Olympics.

• 42 •

NO ONE CAN SAY FOR SURE WHETHER DONOVAN MCNABB THREW UP ON THE FIELD DURING SUPER BOWL XXXIX...BUT WE DEFINITELY KNOW THAT GARY LINEKER POOPED HIS PANTS DURING A GAME IN THE 1990 WORLD CUP.

Lineker was sick, but tried to tough it out anyway. Despite his, err, "accident," Lineker stayed in the game!

43. WILT CHAMBERLAIN CLAIMED TO HAVE SLEPT WITH 20,000 WOMEN DURING HIS LIFETIME.

It's probably bullshit, but who knows? Wilt was one of the most talented players to ever play the game.

44. KOBE BRYANT'S PARENTS HAD TO CO-SIGN HIS FIRST NBA CONTRACT.

Kobe was drafted straight out of high school, and was technically still a minor at the time. He couldn't sign his own contract until he turned 18!

45. MLB MANAGER ALVIN DARK ONCE SAID, "THERE'LL BE A MAN ON THE MOON BEFORE [PITCHER] GAYLORD PERRY HITS A HOME RUN." PERRY HIT HIS FIRST CAREER HOME RUN LESS THAN AN HOUR AFTER NEIL ARMSTRONG SAID HIS FAMOUS WORDS.

It's tough to know whether this story is entirely true, but Alvin Dark never denied it. Let's all choose to believe!

46. TRUE OR FALSE: OVER 10,000 HOT AIR BALLOONS PARTICIPATE IN THE ALBUQUERQUE INTERNATIONAL BALLOON FIESTA EACH YEAR.

False. Albuquerque DOES host a hot air balloon festival, but participation is usually around 500 balloonists.

47. TRUE OR FALSE: A CITY IN SCOTLAND HOSTS AN ANNUAL "CHEESE ROLLING FESTIVAL."

True! Participants chase wheels of cheese down a hill. The goal is to catch the cheese, but it's highly unlikely that you will. The hill is so steep that the cheese wheels can roll at over 50 MPH!

48. TRUE OR FALSE: THE WORLD RECORD FOR FASTEST BOXING KNOCKOUT IS JUST TWO SECONDS.

True! Ryohei Masuda set the record in 2008 after his opponent opened the bout by sprinting directly at him.

• 49 •

TRUE OR FALSE: FORMER NFL PLAYER CHAD JOHNSON CHALLENGED A HORSE TO A RACE... AND WON.

True. The stunt was part of a reality television show, but Johnson's victory over the horse was very real.

50. TRUE OR FALSE: JAI ALAI PLAYERS CAN WHIP THE BALL ALMOST AS FAST AS MLB PITCHERS.

False. In fact, in a Jai Alai game, the ball can move significantly faster than a baseball. The ball often reaches speeds of over 175 MPH, which allows Jai Alai to market itself as "the fastest sport in the world."

51. TRUE OR FALSE: THE LONGEST TENNIS MATCH IN HISTORY LASTED OVER 11 HOURS OF PLAY.

True. John Isner and Nicolas Mahut were forced into a tiebreaker during the fifth and final set. While a tiebreaker would usually add a few extra minutes to a match, this one added hours, finally finishing with an astonishing 70-68 score (Isner won).

52. TRUE OR FALSE: THE RECORD FOR CONSECUTIVE NO-HITTERS IN MAJOR LEAGUE BASEBALL IS THREE.

Sadly, this one is false. However, Johnny Vander Meer is the only pitcher in history to throw two no-hitters in a row.

53. TRUE OR FALSE: 36 RED CARDS WERE ONCE ISSUED IN A SINGLE SOCCER MATCH.

True. The match took place in Paraguay, and when fighting between the players escalated into an all-out brawl, the referees tossed every single player (both the starting lineup and substitutes) from the match.

54. TRUE OR FALSE: THE FASTEST HAT TRICK IN NHL HISTORY TOOK JUST UNDER TWO MINUTES TO COMPLETE.

False. Incredibly, Bill Mosienko scored three goals in just 21 SECONDS during a 1952 game against the New York Rangers. It's a record that is unlikely to be broken anytime soon.

55. TRUE OR FALSE: TIGER WOODS STILL HOLDS THE RECORD FOR MOST CONSECUTIVE PGA TOUR WINS.

False. In fact, Tiger never even came close to the record. While Tiger's seven straight wins are impressive, Byron Nelson won 11 consecutive events in 1945.

TRUE OR FALSE: MUHAMMAD ALI ONCE FOUGHT SUPERMAN.

True! Well, as true as it can be. DC Comics published a comic featuring a fictional fight between Ali and the Man of Steel (spoiler alert: Ali won).

57. TRUE OR FALSE: AN NBA PLAYER ONCE AVERAGED MORE MINUTES PER GAME THAN THERE ARE MINUTES IN AN NBA GAME.

True. Wilt Chamberlain (who else?) averaged 48.5 minutes per game in 1961-62. That means he played every minute of every game…PLUS every minute of every overtime. Truly a record that will never be broken.

58. TRUE OR FALSE: NO PLAYER IN MLB HISTORY HAS EVER HIT TWO GRAND SLAMS IN ONE INNING.

False. In 1999, Fernando Tatis became the only player to accomplish this feat. In doing so, he also set the Major League Baseball record for RBIs in a single inning.

59. TRUE OR FALSE: LEGENDARY COACH PAT SUMMITT NEVER HAD A LOSING RECORD DURING HER ENTIRE COACHING CAREER.

True. Summitt had an astonishing 38 consecutive winning seasons, never once leading the Tennessee Lady Vols to a losing record.

60. TRUE OR FALSE: NO NBA PLAYER HAS EVER AVERAGED A TRIPLE-DOUBLE FOR AN ENTIRE SEASON.

LEBRON JAMES HAS JUST A FEW MORE TRIPLE-DOUBLES IN HIS ENTIRE CAREER THAN ROBERTSON HAD IN THIS ONE SEASON!

False. Oscar Robertson accomplished this insane feat in 1962. Triple-doubles (achieving double digits in three scoring categories) are rare in basketball.

61. TRUE OR FALSE: LEGENDARY 49ERS QUARTERBACK STEVE YOUNG CAN TRACE HIS LINEAGE DIRECTLY BACK TO GEORGE WASHINGTON.

False. But he CAN trace his lineage back to Brigham Young, one of the most important figures in the Mormon Church.

62. TRUE OR FALSE: PITTSBURGH IS THE ONLY CITY WHERE EVERY ONE OF ITS PROFESSIONAL SPORTS TEAMS WEARS THE SAME COLORS.

True. Pittsburgh has a football, hockey, and baseball team...all of which wear black and yellow.

• 63 •

TRUE OR FALSE: MAJOR LEAGUE BASEBALL USES ABOUT 900,000 BALLS EVERY SEASON.

True. According to the league's best estimate, anyway.

64. TRUE OR FALSE: THE SILHOUETTE ON THE NBA LEAGUE LOGO IS ACTUALLY MICHAEL JORDAN.

False. It is actually former Laker Jerry West, who has become affectionately known as "The Logo."

65. TRUE OR FALSE: THE FIRST CHEERLEADING SQUAD WASN'T ORGANIZED UNTIL 1972.

False. Cheerleading actually dates back to the University of Minnesota in 1898!

66. TRUE OR FALSE: FRISBEE REMAINS THE ONLY SPORT EVER PLAYED ON THE MOON.

False. Astronauts have played golf on the moon...but never frisbee. At least not yet!

67. TRUE OR FALSE: THE NFL ONCE SPENT TWO YEARS BATTLING A TEAM IN COURT OVER THE AIR PRESSURE IN ITS FOOTBALLS.

Sadly true. As insane as it sounds, NFL Commissioner Roger Goodell took the New England Patriots to task over an alleged air pressure infraction. Although the NFL never managed to prove that the Patriots committed any infraction in the first place, that did not stop Goodell from harshly punishing the team.

68. TRUE OR FALSE: EARLY FOOTBALLS WERE MADE OUT OF PIG SKINS.

False. Even though the football is colloquially referred to as "the pigskin," it has never actually been made from pig skins.

69. TRUE OR FALSE: IT IS IMPOSSIBLE TO FINISH AN NFL GAME WITH NEGATIVE PASSING YARDS.

False. Since sacks count as negative passing yardage and players can run backwards after catching the ball, it has happened multiple times. The lowest passing yardage total in history came in 1967, when the Denver Broncos passed for -57 yards against the Oakland Raiders.

70. TRUE OR FALSE: LEGENDARY LAKERS PLAYER JERRY WEST HAS WON MORE NBA CHAMPIONSHIPS THAN ANY OTHER PLAYER.

False. Despite being one of the greatest players in NBA history, West went a miserable 1-8 in the NBA finals.

71. TRUE OR FALSE: LEGENDARY QUARTERBACK JOE NAMATH ONCE DONNED PANTYHOSE FOR A TELEVISION COMMERCIAL.

True. The commercial became one of the most famous of all time.

72. TRUE OR FALSE: THE FIRST VOLLEYBALL WAS ACTUALLY A BASKETBALL.

True...mostly. The inventor of the sport removed the hard skin of the basketball, leaving just the soft inner bladder. Later, a new ball would be created specifically for the sport.

73. TRUE OR FALSE: OLYMPIC GOLD MEDALS ARE NOT MADE OF GOLD.

True...and it's even worse than you think. They're actually made of silver!

74. TRUE OR FALSE: IT IS POSSIBLE FOR A BASEBALL PLAYER TO BE TRADED FOR HIMSELF.

True. It has happened four times in history. Since baseball allows the inclusion of "a player to be named later" in trades, it leaves open the possibility that the aforementioned player could be the original player included in the trade!

75. TRUE OR FALSE: IN THE NBA, A JUMP BALL USED TO FOLLOW EVERY MADE BASKET.

True. Thankfully this rule was changed in the 1930s to prevent games from lasting eight hours.

76. TRUE OR FALSE: JAMIE MOYER IS THE OLDEST PLAYER TO APPEAR IN AN MLB GAME, HAVING PITCHED UNTIL THE AGE OF 49.

False. Famed pitcher Satchel Paige appeared in a regular season Major League Baseball game at the age of 59.

77. TRUE OR FALSE: ALTHOUGH JFK'S GOLF CLUBS SOLD FOR $20,000 ON *SEINFELD*, IN REAL LIFE THEY FETCHED JUST OVER $12,000.

False. JFK's golf clubs (split into two lots) were sold for over $1.1 million at auction in 1996.

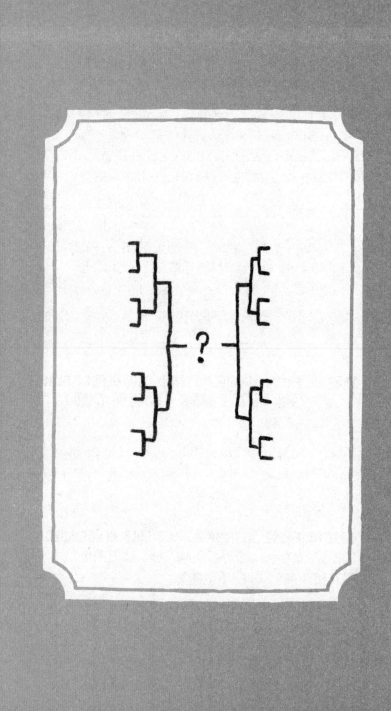

· 78 ·

TRUE OR FALSE: ONLY ONE PERSON HAS EVER RECORDED A PERFECT MARCH MADNESS BRACKET.

False. It has never been done. In fact, it is so statistically improbable that it may NEVER be done!

79. TRUE OR FALSE: BASEBALL TEAMS USED TO WEAR SHORTS.

False...with one exception. Famed owner Bill Veeck once had his Chicago White Sox wear shorts as part of a promotion. Unsurprisingly, the stunt was not repeated.

80. TRUE OR FALSE: THE "GORDIE HOWE HAT TRICK" IN HOCKEY REFERS TO SCORING A GOAL, AN ASSIST, AND A PENALTY SHOT.

False. A Gordie Howe Hat Trick refers to scoring a goal, recording an assist, and getting into a fight.

81. TRUE OR FALSE: A BASEBALL GAME CONTAINS LESS THAN 20 MINUTES OF ACTUAL GAME ACTION.

True. Despite routinely lasting more than three hours, baseball games usually only contain about 15 to 18 minutes of actual action.

84. TRUE OR FALSE: THE NATIONAL SPORT OF AFGHANISTAN IS BUZKASHI, A DERIVATIVE OF AMERICAN BASEBALL.

False. Buzkashi is Persian for "goat grabbing," and the sport involves attempting to move a goat carcass across a goal line.

83. TRUE OR FALSE: ONE OF THE GREATEST PITCHERS IN MLB HISTORY USED TO RUN OFF THE FIELD DURING GAMES TO CHASE FIRE TRUCKS.

True. "Rube" Waddell had a fascination with fire trucks, and managers had a difficult time keeping him on the mound if one drove by. That didn't stop Waddell from being one of the greatest strikeout pitchers in the history of Major League Baseball.

85. TRUE OR FALSE: GOLFER ARNOLD PALMER REALLY DID INVENT THE "ARNOLD PALMER" DRINK.

True. While people had surely been mixing iced tea and lemonade for many years, Palmer drank it regularly and can be credited with popularizing the mixture.

86. TRUE OR FALSE: EVEN HORSES ARE TESTED FOR PEDS AT THE OLYMPICS.

True. And they have tested positive more than once!

87. TRUE OR FALSE: TODAY'S STANLEY CUP DATES BACK TO 1892, DINGS, DENTS, AND ALL!

False. The Stanley Cup awarded today is actually the second iteration of the trophy (with a third that serves as a stand-in when the real Cup isn't available).

· 88 ·

TRUE OR FALSE: "WIFE CARRYING" IS A SPORT IN NORTH AMERICA.

True. The North American Wife Carrying Championship has been held annually since 1999.

89. TRUE OR FALSE: NO ATHLETE HAS EVER WON GOLD MEDALS AT BOTH THE SUMMER AND WINTER OLYMPICS.

False. USA boxer/bobsledder Eddie Eagan won gold in the 1920 Summer and 1932 Winter Olympics.

90. TRUE OR FALSE: OLYMPIC ATHLETES USED TO COMPETE IN THE NUDE.

True. In ancient Greece, competitors were expected to be nude during all events. Fortunately (unfortunately?), that has changed in modern times.

91. TRUE OR FALSE: TOM BRADY (PICK #199) WAS THE LOWEST-DRAFTED QUARTERBACK TO LEAD HIS TEAM TO A SUPER BOWL VICTORY.

False. In fact, several Super Bowl winning quarterbacks were drafted lower than Brady. Brad Johnson was drafted #227, and Kurt Warner was not drafted at all! Steve Young was also not drafted, but this was because he elected to join the United States Football League instead of the NFL—otherwise, he would have been a top pick.

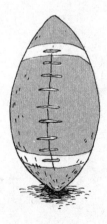

HISTORY AND POLITICS THROUGH THE LENS OF
the Bizarre

They say that those who don't learn from history are doomed to repeat it. Maybe we should be so lucky as to repeat some of these ridiculous episodes from history. After all, politics has become so crazy today that we often forget just how ridiculous it was in the past. Crazy laws. Insane political candidates. State birds and flowers that don't make a lick of sense. If you know where to look, you'll never lack for crazy stories in your state, your country, or the rest of the world.

So take heart! No matter how wild and weird things get today, you can always rest assured that someone somewhere was weirder, wackier, and crazier. The best part? Some of these crazy facts still stand to this day!

1. THE STATE SPORT OF MARYLAND IS JOUSTING.

2. HAMSTERS ARE ILLEGAL IN HAWAII.

Hamsters would thrive in the Hawaiian climate, and Hawaiian lawmakers fear the effects that introducing a new species into the delicate ecosystem there could have.

3. RICHARD NIXON REALLY WANTED TO BE A RAPPER.

He was once quoted as saying, "I have often thought that if there had been a good rap group around in those days, I might have chosen a career in music instead of politics."

4. AUDIE MURPHY IS ONE OF THE MOST DECORATED SOLDIERS IN AMERICAN HISTORY.

Although he later became famous as a Hollywood actor, Audie Murphy served in World War II and was awarded over 30 different medals for valor from the U.S. military.

5. AS MANY AS 750,000 AMERICANS ARE ESTIMATED TO HAVE DIED IN THE CIVIL WAR—ALMOST 2.5% OF THE TOTAL POPULATION OF THE COUNTRY AT THE TIME.

6. AT THE HEIGHT OF HIS POWER, COLOMBIAN CARTEL BOSS PABLO ESCOBAR WAS SPENDING $2,500 PER WEEK ON RUBBER BANDS TO HOLD THE MONEY HE WAS BRINGING IN.

It is also estimated that the cartel lost about $2.1 billion per year to rats eating the money in storage.

7. THE CONTINENT WITH THE HIGHEST LITERACY RATE IS ANTARCTICA.

Since the only people living on Antarctica are scientific researchers, it makes sense that the adult literacy rate is 100%!

8. THE BROTHER OF JOHN WILKES BOOTHE ONCE SAVED THE LIFE OF ABRAHAM LINCOLN'S SON.

9. THE "EMU WAR" IS A REAL WAR THAT TOOK PLACE IN AUSTRALIA. EMUS WERE THE ENEMY.

The "war" was waged to curb the emu population in Australia. Unfortunately for many Australians, the emus won.

• 10 •

CLEOPATRA'S REIGN WAS CLOSER TO THE MOON LANDING THAN THE BUILDING OF THE PYRAMIDS.

11. UNCONFIRMED REPORTS SUGGEST THAT DURING THE COLD WAR, THE CIA PLANNED TO DEMORALIZE THE SOVIET PEOPLE BY AIR DROPPING THOUSANDS OF MAGNUM-SIZED AMERICAN CONDOMS LABELED "SMALL."

12. THE CIA USED CATS AS SPIES.

According to a former CIA agent, the CIA surgically implanted cats with listening equipment and released them around sensitive Soviet locations during the Cold War.

ALTHOUGH THE CIA DENIES IT, EVIDENCE SUGGESTS THAT THE FIRST OF THESE CATS WAS IMMEDIATELY HIT BY A CAR AND KILLED.

13. ALBERT EINSTEIN COULD HAVE BECOME THE PRESIDENT OF ISRAEL.

In 1952, Israel offered him the presidency. Although the presidency is a largely symbolic position in Israel, the country's first president reportedly considered Einstein the "greatest Jew alive."

14. OXFORD UNIVERSITY PREDATES THE AZTECS BY CENTURIES.

Oxford University has been around since 1096. The Aztec Empire didn't rise to power until 1428.

15. SAUDI ARABIA IMPORTS SAND.

The quality of Saudi Arabia's sand is too poor to make glass, so they have to import it from other sandy countries.

16. ADOLF HITLER WAS ONCE NOMINATED FOR A NOBEL PEACE PRIZE.

In 1939, a member of the Swedish Parliament submitted the nomination, although, according to him, it was not intended to be a serious nomination—more of a way to make a point.

17. THE UNITED STATES HAS COME DANGEROUSLY CLOSE TO ACCIDENTALLY NUKING ITSELF.

In 1961, two nuclear warheads were actually dropped on the state of North Carolina when the plane that carried them came apart in midair. Luckily, neither exploded. Today the place where they came to rest is indicated by a historic mile marker.

• 18 •

THE ONLY TREE IN THE SAHARA DESERT WAS KILLED BY A DRUNK DRIVER IN 1973.

Alright, so it wasn't the only tree in the entire Sahara. But the Tree of Ténéré was the only tree for 250 miles in any direction, and an allegedly drunk driver managed to knock it down once and for all.

19. AUTO MANUFACTURER HENRY FORD WAS GIVEN THE HIGHEST HONOR THAT NAZI GERMANY COULD BESTOW UPON A FOREIGNER.

Ford continued to do business with Nazi Germany, and made a fortune producing vehicles for both the Axis and Allied countries. This should come as little surprise, as Ford had a reputation for anti-Semitism.

20. IN THE EARLY DAYS OF AUTOMOBILES, ENGLAND REQUIRED THAT A MAN CARRYING A RED FLAG MUST WALK AHEAD TO WARN PEDESTRIANS.

To accommodate this, the speed limit was just 2 miles per hour in the city and 4 miles per hour in the country.

21. THE SMITHSONIAN ARCHIVES ALLEGEDLY HOLD A JAR CONTAINING A RUBBER MOLD OF JOHN DILLINGER'S PENIS.

The jar's origins are unknown, but Dillinger was widely believed to have possessed an enormous penis, a legend that has survived well past his death. The "synthetic polymer" is believed to be someone's idea of a joke.

22. THE WRIGHT BROTHERS' FIRST FLIGHT TOOK PLACE IN 1903. IT TOOK US JUST 66 MORE YEARS TO LAND ON THE MOON.

23. IN 1868, THE DEMOCRATIC PARTY FORCED AN UNWILLING CANDIDATE TO ACCEPT THEIR NOMINATION FOR PRESIDENT.

The awesomely-named Horatio Seymour repeatedly made it known that he had no interest in running for president, but he was unanimously drafted at the party convention and forced to campaign. Unsurprisingly, he lost to Ulysses S. Grant.

24. THE U.S. COULD HAVE HAD A PRESIDENT NAMED WENDELL WILLKIE.

Although he sounds like a Peter Sellers character, Wendell Willkie ran against FDR in 1940, despite being a staunch supporter of most of FDR's policies.

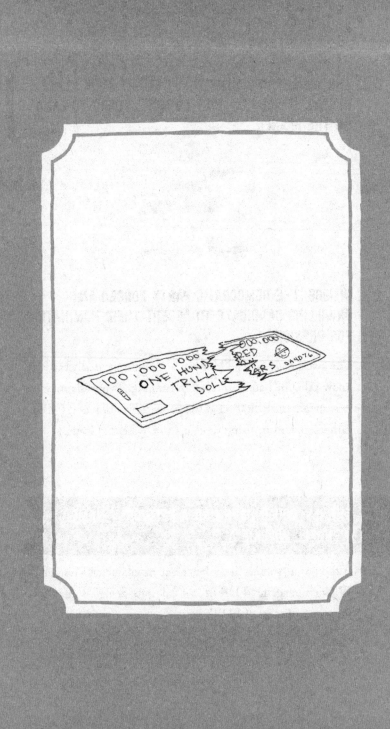

• 25 •

HYPERINFLATION IN ZIMBABWE GOT SO BAD IN THE EARLY 2000S THAT 100 TRILLION DOLLAR BILLS WERE COMMONPLACE.

The currency is now defunct, but you can buy surviving bills online if you're looking for an interesting souvenir.

26. DURING A COMMITTEE HEARING, U.S. CONGRESSMAN HANK JOHNSON ONCE ASKED WHETHER GUAM COULD BECOME SO OVERPOPULATED THAT IT MIGHT "TIP OVER AND CAPSIZE." IN 2010.

He has been re-elected several times since then.

27. IN THE LATE 1800S, TWO PALEONTOLOGISTS BRUTALLY BATTLED EACH OTHER FOR DINOSAUR BONES IN WHAT HAS BECOME KNOWN AS "THE BONE WARS."

The pair of scholars stole from each other, bribed officials for dig rights, and waged heated battles in the press. Over dinosaur bones!

28. AT ONE TIME, PEOPLE THOUGHT TUBERCULOSIS SUFFERERS WERE VAMPIRES.

29. JOHNNY APPLESEED WAS A REAL PERSON.

His real name was John Chapman, and he really did introduce apple trees to large parts of America!

30. THE UNITED STATES BOUGHT ALASKA FROM RUSSIA FOR A PRICE THAT EQUATED TO UNDER 2 CENTS PER ACRE.

31. GENERAL SANTA ANNA ORDERED HIS AMPUTATED LEG TO BE BURIED WITH FULL MILITARY HONORS.

Hey, when you're the boss, you can do what you want.

32. NAPOLEON WAS NOT ACTUALLY SHORT.

It was actually foreign propagandists who managed to perpetuate this myth in order to reduce Napoleon to a comic character. While today we might consider Napoleon (now believed to be 5'6" or 5'7") short, he was actually taller than the average Frenchman at the time.

33. INTERRACIAL MARRIAGE WAS NOT LEGALIZED IN THE UNITED STATES UNTIL 1967.

The next time someone tells you that racism was "way in the past," feel free to share this fact with them.

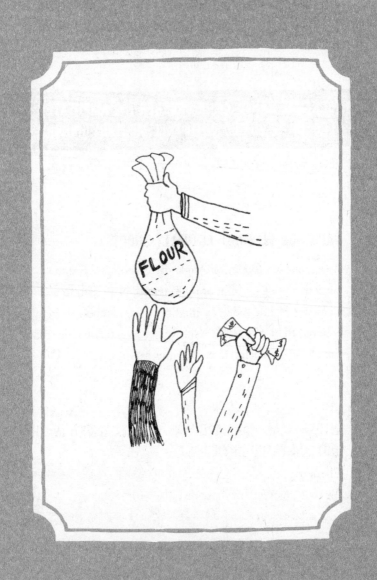

• 34 •

A SINGLE BAG OF FLOUR WAS ONCE SOLD FOR $275,000...IN THE 1860S!

The bag was used as a symbol and was repeatedly sold at auction to raise money for charity.

35. AT ITS PEAK, THE MONGOL EMPIRE ENCOMPASSED OVER ¼ OF THE WORLD'S POPULATION.

36. AS RECENTLY AS THE EIGHTEENTH CENTURY, THE AVERAGE HEIGHT OF A HUMAN MAN WAS ABOUT 5'6".

Humans have gotten significantly taller over time—today the average male height is 5'10".

37. TEDDY ROOSEVELT WAS ONCE SHOT IN THE MIDDLE OF DELIVERING A SPEECH. HE FINISHED THE SPEECH.

38. STALIN WAS EDITING PHOTOS LONG BEFORE COMPUTERS.

When Stalin would have a member of his inner circle eliminated, he would erase them from all photographic evidence. There are numerous examples of photographs containing Stalin alongside multiple advisors who would dwindle one by one as time went on.

39. PRESIDENT LYNDON B. JOHNSON HAD THE WHITE HOUSE SHOWERS MODIFIED TO SHOOT A JET OF WATER DIRECTLY AT HIS PENIS.

Although it is difficult to verify much of what unofficially goes on in the White House, Kate Andersen Brower's book *The Residence: Inside the Private World of the White House* includes this interesting tidbit.

40. TRUE OR FALSE: THE BLACK DEATH KILLED ALMOST A QUARTER OF THE PEOPLE IN EUROPE.

False. The Black Death killed a THIRD of Europe's population…and it did it in just five years.

41. TRUE OR FALSE: THE SLANG TERM "HOOKER," REFERRING TO A PROSTITUTE, ORIGINATED WITH CIVIL WAR GENERAL JOSEPH HOOKER.

False, although it is a popular rumor. General Hooker kept his men so well supplied with prostitutes that his men were credited with coining the term. However, linguists have found evidence that the word was used well before General Hooker's time.

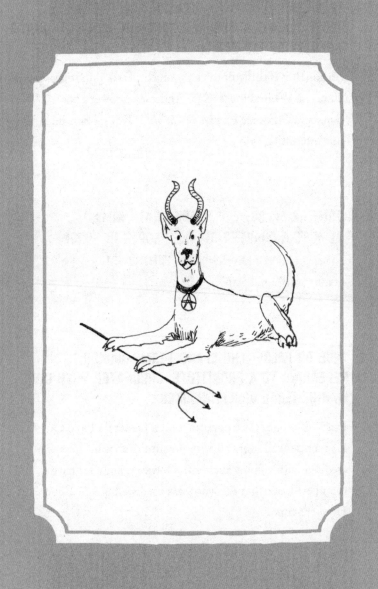

· 42 ·

TRUE OR FALSE: PRESIDENT JOHN ADAMS HAD A DOG NAMED JESUS.

False…but he did have a dog named Satan.

43. **TRUE OR FALSE: THE SECOND MAN ON THE MOON, BUZZ ALDRIN, WOULD GO ON TO BECOME A RAPPER.**

True…sort of. Aldrin recorded a sort-of rap song with Snoop Dogg as his producer. The song was called "The Rocket Experience."

44. **TRUE OR FALSE: IVAN THE TERRIBLE WAS THE INSPIRATION FOR DRACULA.**

False. Actually, Vlad the Impaler gets that ignominious distinction.

45. **TRUE OR FALSE: ROMAN EMPEROR CALIGULA APPOINTED HIS HORSE TO THE SENATE.**

False. Although Caligula was known for pampering his horses to the extreme, the idea that he appointed his horse to the Senate actually originates in the novel *I, Claudius*.

46. **TRUE OR FALSE: SOVIET SCIENTISTS ONCE TRIED TO CREATE A HUMAN/CHIMPANZEE HYBRID.**

True. Fortunately (unfortunately?) they were unable to impregnate the chimpanzee with human sperm.

47. TRUE OR FALSE: THE POPE ONCE WROTE A ROMANCE NOVEL.

True. Although he wasn't the Pope at the time of its publication, Pope Pius II wrote a romance novel titled *The Tale of the Two Lovers*.

48. TRUE OR FALSE: IN THE ROMAN EMPIRE, HORSE URINE WAS USED AS MOUTHWASH.

False. The truth is so much worse. They actually used HUMAN urine.

49. TRUE OR FALSE: CONFEDERATE GENERAL ROBERT E. LEE DIDN'T OWN SLAVES, BUT UNION GENERAL ULYSSES S. GRANT DID.

True. Grant was not a prolific slave owner, but he did own one slave.

50. TRUE OR FALSE: THE UNITED STATES GOVERNMENT POISONED BEER DURING PROHIBITION.

True. The government's overzealous attempt to curb alcohol consumption in the US resulted in more than a few deaths.

· 51 ·

TRUE OR FALSE: THE FIRST BOMB THAT THE ALLIES DROPPED ON GERMANY DURING WWII KILLED AN ELEPHANT.

True. In fact, it killed several: the bomb fell on the Berlin Zoo and killed seven of the zoo's eight elephants.

52. TRUE OR FALSE: ENGLISH IS THE OFFICIAL LANGUAGE OF ALL 50 STATES.

False. Despite what many believe, the United States does not have an official language.

53. TRUE OR FALSE: ONE PASSENGER WAS ABOARD BOTH THE TITANIC AND ITS SISTER SHIP BRITANNIC WHEN THEY WERE SUNK.

True. Violet Jessop was aboard both ships and survived both disasters.

54. TRUE OR FALSE: JULIUS CAESAR WAS ONCE KIDNAPPED BY PIRATES, BUT ESCAPED BEFORE HIS RANSOM COULD BE PAID.

False. Not only did the Romans pay the ransom, but also Caesar was insulted by the pirates' original request of 20 pieces of silver and demanded that they increase it to 50.

55. TRUE OR FALSE: ABOUT 5% OF THE WORLD'S POPULATION CAN TRACE ITS LINEAGE BACK TO GENGHIS KHAN.

False. But Khan's proliferation is still impressive: about 1 in 200 people are said to be descended from the legendary warlord. In Asia, the number rises as high as 8%!

56. TRUE OR FALSE: THE SWASTIKA USED TO BE SEEN AS A POSITIVE SYMBOL.

True. The Nazis co-opted the symbol when the rose to power, and have made a once-straightforward symbol of good fortune incredibly complicated to look back on.

57. TRUE OR FALSE: UNTIL RECENTLY, RUSSIA DID NOT CONSIDER BEER TO BE AN ALCOHOLIC DRINK.

True. Anything containing less than 10% alcohol was considered a soft drink in Russia until 2011.

58. TRUE OR FALSE: MORE THAN 20 BOSTONIANS DROWNED IN A WAVE OF ALCOHOL IN 1919.

False. But 21 people did die in a molasses wave after a tank ruptured due to high heat.

59. TRUE OR FALSE: IT WAS COMMONPLACE FOR WOMEN TO WEAR PANTS AS FAR BACK AS THE 1700S.

False. It was not common to see women wearing pants until the twentieth century.

TRUE OR FALSE: THE POPE ONCE DECLARED BLACK CATS TO BE AN INCARNATION OF SATAN.

True. Pope Gregory IX believed that black cats were tied to the devil, which caused many followers to shun or even kill cats. Some believe that the lack of cats to keep the rat population in check may even have contributed to the spread of the Bubonic Plague.

61. TRUE OR FALSE: THE NAME "JESSICA" WAS INVENTED BY SHAKESPEARE.

True. The oldest recorded instance of the name was in Shakespeare's play *The Merchant of Venice*.

62. TRUE OR FALSE: THE RUSSIANS DID NOT SUFFER A SINGLE CASUALTY DURING THE SIEGE OF STALINGRAD.

False. Russian losses during the siege outnumbered all casualties suffered by the U.S. and U.K. during the entire war.

63. TRUE OR FALSE: THE FIRST LEADER OF AN INDEPENDENT CHILE WAS IRISH.

True. And his name was Bernardo O'Higgins!

64. TRUE OR FALSE: HITLER HAD A NEPHEW WHO FOUGHT AGAINST HIM IN WORLD WAR II.

True. William Hitler (who later changed his name to William Stuart-Houston) served in the U.S. Navy during the war.

65. TRUE OR FALSE: THE WHISKEY REBELLION REALLY WAS FOUGHT OVER WHISKEY.

True. Taxes had been raised on whiskey, putting small-time distributors at a great economic disadvantage.

66. TRUE OR FALSE: IN THE PAST, DENTURES WERE ONLY USED BY CORPSES TO MAKE THEM APPEAR AS HEALTHY AS POSSIBLE IN DEATH.

False. Actually, teeth were often pulled from corpses to make dentures for the living.

67. TRUE OR FALSE: THE MAYANS NEVER ACTUALLY REMOVED THE BEATING HEARTS OF THEIR HUMAN SACRIFICES.

False. This is one rumor that turns out to be true!

68. TRUE OR FALSE: THE HUNDRED YEARS' WAR ACTUALLY LASTED JUST UNDER 100 YEARS.

False. The war lasted 116 years.

• 69 •

TRUE OR FALSE: CATHERINE THE GREAT HAD AN ENTIRE ROOM FILLED WITH EROTIC FURNITURE.

True. The entire room was said to be filled with items of furniture emblazoned with penises and vaginas.

70. TRUE OR FALSE: THE *GETTYSBURG ADDRESS* WAS NOT THE KEYNOTE SPEECH OF THE EVENT.

True. The keynote was delivered by Edward Everett. Unlike Lincoln's brief speech, Everett's lasted upwards of two hours!

71. TRUE OR FALSE: BRUTUS SLEPT WITH THE MOTHER OF JULIUS CAESAR.

False. Other way 'round! Brutus's mother was one of Caesar's mistresses. No wonder he was mad.

72. TRUE OR FALSE: MOUNT RUSHMORE HAS ONLY BEEN AROUND SINCE 1972.

False. Mount Rushmore was completed in 1939.

73. TRUE OR FALSE: THE AUSTRIAN ARMY ONCE MISTAKENLY ATTACKED ITSELF.

True. The Battle of Karánsebes reportedly resulted in losses of up to 10,000 soldiers when one Austrian regiment mistook another for the enemy.

74. TRUE OR FALSE: IN THE LATE 1800S, RUSSIAN SEPARATISTS ATTEMPTED TO CREATE A "NEW RUSSIA" IN SOUTH AMERICA.

False. But the Australians did! New Australia was a colony in Paraguay founded in 1893.

75. TRUE OR FALSE: MORE THAN 1% OF THE U.S. POPULATION IS CURRENTLY IN JAIL.

False. But it's not far off. Estimates place the percentage of Americans in jail at any one time at 0.9%.

A POTPOURRI OF
Facts That Don't Fit

Some of the craziest facts out there defy classification. And that's probably a good thing. After all, why try to cram crazy into a box? Just let it run free! Odd inventions, geographical quirks, and weird individuals can all tickle the funny bone and stimulate the mind in their own way.

These are the facts that don't really fit. They aren't about nature, and they aren't about sports. They didn't start a war, and they don't orbit another star. These weirdos just don't fit in—and we love them for it.

1. THE SPORT OF "HORSE DIVING" ONCE ATTRACTED CROWDS OF SPECTATORS SO LARGE THAT THEY CAUSED STEEL PIER IN ATLANTIC CITY, NJ, TO SINK.

The pier didn't sink all the way—in fact, the change was almost imperceptible until scientists noticed a pattern in the sea level readings generated by a sensor on the pier. In the end, almost 50 years of sea level data had to be thrown out, all thanks to diving horses.

2. THE CAN OPENER WASN'T INVENTED UNTIL NEARLY 50 YEARS AFTER THE CAN.

3. WHEN YOU RECEIVE A KIDNEY TRANSPLANT, THE DOCTORS USUALLY LEAVE THE ORIGINAL KIDNEY INSIDE OF YOU.

A surprising number of people are walking around with three kidneys! The old kidney is only removed if leaving it in poses a specific danger to the patient.

4. MORE PEOPLE ARE KILLED BY VENDING MACHINES EACH YEAR THAN SHARKS.

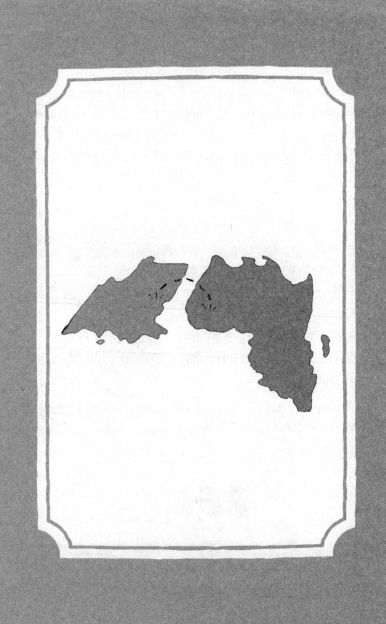

• 5 •

SHOCKINGLY, THE U.S. STATE CLOSEST TO AFRICA ISN'T FLORIDA—IT'S MAINE!

6. IF THERE ARE 23 PEOPLE IN A ROOM, THERE IS A 50% CHANCE THAT TWO OF THEM SHARE A BIRTHDAY.

Statisticians call this "The Birthday Paradox." If there are 75 people in a room, there is a 99.9% chance that two share a birthday.

7. HUMANS LANDED ON THE MOON BEFORE INVENTING WHEELED SUITCASES.

While the first moon landing occurred in 1969, the patent for the first rolling luggage wasn't filed until 1970.

THAT MEANS THAT WHILE NEIL ARMSTRONG AND BUZZ ALDRIN MAY HAVE BEEN AMAZING PIONEERS, THEY STILL HAD TO CARRY THEIR OVERNIGHT BAGS ONTO THE ROCKET.

8. THE LIGHTER WAS INVENTED BEFORE THE MATCH.

The earliest lighter was known as a Döbereiner's lamp and was invented in 1823 (although if you count the lighting mechanism in a flintlock pistol, the invention dates back even earlier). Friction matches like the ones we use today were not invented until 1826.

9. WHEN FUTURE VIDEO GAME COMPANY NINTENDO WAS FOUNDED, THE OTTOMAN EMPIRE WAS STILL A MAJOR POWER IN EUROPE.

Nintendo was founded in 1889. The Ottoman Empire would not dissolve until 1922.

10. THE CAPITAL OF NEVADA IS WEST OF LOS ANGELES.

In fact, there are not one, not two, but six U.S. state capitals west of Los Angeles. They are Juneau, AK; Honolulu, HI; Carson City, NV; Salem, OR; Olympia, WA; and Sacramento, CA.

11. THE PEOPLE OF LOS ANGELES ARE SO ACCUSTOMED TO LIGHT POLLUTION THAT WHEN AN EARTHQUAKE CAUSED A BLACKOUT IN 1994, MANY CITIZENS CALLED OBSERVATORIES TO ASK ABOUT THE WEIRD LIGHTS IN THE SKY. THEY WERE STARS.

12. A MAJORITY OF CANADIANS LIVE SOUTH OF SEATTLE.

Sounds weird, but it's true! Northern Canada is largely wilderness, while southern Canada (particularly the area around the Great Lakes) contains many major metropolises.

13. WHEN YOU PERFORM AN ACTION, NEURONS FIRE IN YOUR BRAIN. THOSE SAME NEURONS FIRE WHEN WATCHING SOMEONE PERFORM THE SAME ACTION.

14. THERE ARE 80,000,000,000,000,000,000,000,000,000, 000,000,000,000,000,000,000,000,000,000,000,000,000 WAYS TO ARRANGE A DECK OF CARDS.

That means there are more ways to arrange a deck of cards than there are atoms on Earth.

DECK O'CARDS

15. STUDIES SUGGEST THAT PLACEBOS WORK EVEN WHEN THE SUBJECT KNOWS THEY ARE TAKING A PLACEBO.

16. ASTROGLIDE LUBE WAS ORIGINALLY SUPPOSED TO BE SPACE SHUTTLE COOLANT.

Which explains how it earned the name "Astro"-glide!

17. THE CORNISH WORD FOR "BREATH" IS "ANAL."

18. THE DARKEST SUBSTANCE KNOWN IS CALLED "VANTABLACK" AND ABSORBS 99.965% OF ALL VISIBLE LIGHT.

19. SIR ISAAC NEWTON SPENT HUNDREDS AND HUNDREDS OF PAGES TRYING TO PROVE THAT 1+1 = 2.

It actually isn't that unusual for even the simplest mathematical proofs to be startlingly long. Several hundred pages of Newton's *Principia Mathematica* are dedicated to proving what seems like the most basic of mathematical facts.

20. SOMEONE ONCE LEFT A CAT $12.5 MILLION.

21. THE LETTERS IN "ELEVEN PLUS TWO" CAN BE REARRANGED TO SPELL "TWELVE PLUS ONE."

· 22 ·

THERE IS AN AMERICAN BREWER WHO MAKES A BEER USING YEAST FROM HIS OWN BEARD.

The brewery notes that using unusual yeast strains like this is nothing new for brewers, but it's certainly a shock for most beer drinkers!

23. **ACCORDING TO THE FOUNDER OF MATCH.COM, HE LOST HIS GIRLFRIEND TO ANOTHER MAN...WHO SHE MET ON MATCH.COM.**

24. **SOME CONSPIRACY THEORISTS BELIEVE THAT UP TO THREE HUNDRED YEARS OF HISTORY HAVE BEEN COMPLETELY FABRICATED.**

Adherents to the "Phantom Time Hypothesis" believe that the Holy Roman Empire conspired to add 300 years during the early Middle Ages to the calendar.

25. **SOME PEOPLE ARE AFRAID OF GRAVITY.**

"Barophobia" is a real thing. Some people fear that gravity will crush them, while others fear that they will float away.

26. **"PHOBOPHOBIA" IS A THING.**

And it's exactly what it sounds like. Sufferers are afraid of fear.

28. A MAN IN RUSSIA ONCE GREW A TREE IN HIS LUNG.

Fortunately, doctors were able to remove it before it grew too large. Although some were skeptical of the claim, his doctors were adamant in their belief that he must have accidentally inhaled a seed. Talk about going down the wrong pipe!

29. FAMOUS PHILOSOPHER JEAN-JACQUES ROUSSEAU WAS VERY UP-FRONT ABOUT HIS SEXUAL FETISH: SPANKING.

30. A LIVE CAT WAS ONCE TURNED INTO A TELEPHONE.

It's just as weird as it sounds. By attaching electrodes to a cat's brain and hooking it up to an amplifier, the researchers were able to turn the live animal into a functioning telephone. Did I mention this happened in 1929?

31. TRUE OR FALSE: NUCLEAR FALLOUT USED TO BE MEASURED IN "SUNSHINE UNITS."

True. As weird and dystopian as it sounds, that's the term we used to use. A stand-up comedy bit by George Carlin helped call attention to it and prompted a change.

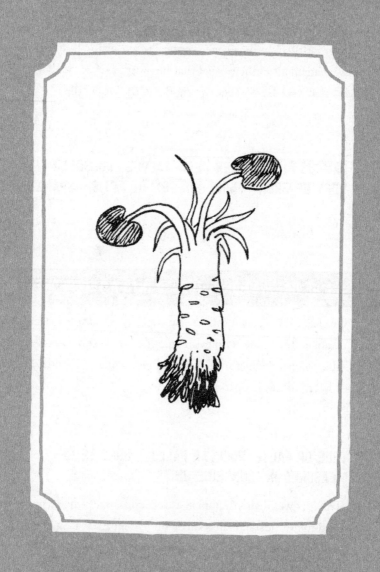

• 32 •

IF YOU ATE NATURAL WASABI, YOU WOULDN'T FIND IT SPICY.

Oddly enough, it only becomes spicy when it is crushed.

33. TRUE OR FALSE: THE VIBRATOR WAS ORIGINALLY INVENTED AS A MEDICAL DEVICE.

True. Orgasms were believed to be able to cure many medical ailments.

34. TRUE OR FALSE: TEA IS BANNED IN THE BRITISH ARMED FORCES.

False. Actually, it's the exact opposite: even British tanks have the ability to make a cup of tea.

35. TRUE OR FALSE: THE HEIMLICH MANEUVER WASN'T INVENTED UNTIL THE 1970S.

True. Henry Heimlich published his first paper on the subject in 1974. Up to that point, choking was primarily dealt with by slapping the victim on the back—a practice that is highly discouraged today.

36. TRUE OR FALSE: MUSICAL INSTRUMENTS WERE NOT INVENTED UNTIL THE EARLY FIFTH CENTURY.

False. The oldest musical instrument ever found dates back 40,000 years. Flutes made of bird bones have been discovered that scientists believe originate 30,000 to 40,000 years in the past.

37. TRUE OR FALSE: CORN FLAKES WERE ORIGINALLY DEVELOPED TO SUPPRESS THE URGE TO MASTURBATE.

True. The Kellogg brothers were deeply religious, and believed that the food would help their brethren suppress the urge to pleasure themselves.

38. TRUE OR FALSE: MORE THAN 200 PEOPLE HAVE DIED ATTEMPTING TO CLIMB MOUNT EVEREST.

True.

39. TRUE OR FALSE: ASPIRIN WAS ORIGINALLY INVENTED TO TREAT ERECTILE DYSFUNCTION.

False. But Viagra was originally invented to treat heart disease.

40. TRUE OR FALSE: THE KAZOO WAS INVENTED BY A MAN NAMED ALABAMA VEST.

True. Although this is a difficult fact to verify, the prevailing belief is that an African American man named Alabama Vest invented the buzzing instrument.

41. TRUE OR FALSE: WHEN DINOSAURS ROAMED THE EARTH, DAYS WERE JUST 23 HOURS LONG.

True. Earth's rotation is slowing over time thanks to the moon's gravitational pull. While there is no consensus on the subject, some scientists believe that during the time of the dinosaurs, a day may have been just 23 hours long.

42. TRUE OR FALSE: WILD HIPPOS CAN ONLY BE FOUND IN AFRICA.

False. They can now be found in Colombia...although this is due to the fact that drug kingpin Pablo Escobar kept hippos as pets. Since his death, they have bred in the wild and become a problem for the country.

43. TRUE OR FALSE: DURING WORLD WAR I, AMERICANS REFERRED TO SAUERKRAUT AS "LIBERTY CABBAGE."

True. Silly as it sounds, "freedom fries" were not the first instance of Americans renaming a food to disparage another country.

· 44 ·

TRUE OR FALSE: CHRISTMAS WAS ORIGINALLY BANNED IN THE AMERICAN COLONIES.

True. The ban was lifted before the American Revolution, but it still took a while to catch on in the states.

45. **TRUE OR FALSE: HUMANS ARE CAPABLE OF ECHOLOCATION.**

True. Although not everyone can do it, some blind people have figured out a way to navigate the world using "clicks," similar to the way that bats navigate in the dark.

46. **TRUE OR FALSE: THERE IS A FOOTBALL FIELD IN THE BASEMENT OF THE U.S. SUPREME COURT BUILDING.**

False. But there is a basketball court on the fifth floor!

47. **TRUE OR FALSE: BENJAMIN FRANKLIN HAS BEEN INDUCTED INTO THE KITE FLYERS HALL OF FAME.**

False. Franklin is a member of the International Swimming Hall of Fame, though!

48. **TRUE OR FALSE: IN THE 1800S, A MAN PROCLAIMED HIMSELF EMPEROR OF THE UNITED STATES AND ISSUED HIS OWN CURRENCY.**

True. Emperor Norton was a (possibly insane) former businessman who was much beloved within the San Francisco community—so much so that the bars and other establishments that he visited would often honor his fake currency.

49. TRUE OR FALSE: LEFT-HANDED PEOPLE LIVE AN AVERAGE OF NINE YEARS LONGER THAN RIGHT-HANDED PEOPLE.

False. Just the opposite, in fact.

50. TRUE OR FALSE: CONSPIRACY THEORISTS BELIEVE THAT A FEMA "DEATH CAMP" IS HIDDEN UNDER LAGUARDIA AIRPORT.

False. That would be ridiculous! Of course, they DO believe that a FEMA death camp is hidden beneath Denver International Airport.

51. TRUE OR FALSE: THERE IS A THEORETICAL PARTICLE THAT MOVES FASTER THAN THE SPEED OF LIGHT.

True. Tachyons are often used in science fiction. They move so quickly that they would essentially appear to move backwards in time.

• 52 •

TRUE OR FALSE: THE NAME "BUTTERFLY" STEMS FROM A TYPO OF THE INSECT'S ORIGINAL NAME, "FLUTTERBY."

False, but this is another myth that has been perpetuated for years and years.

53. TRUE OR FALSE: LEGENDARY CHILDREN'S SHOW HOST MR. ROGERS WAS ONCE A MARINE SNIPER WITH DOZENS OF KILLS UNDER HIS BELT.

False. Despite the popularity of this rumor, there is no evidence that Fred Rogers ever served in the military, let alone as a sniper.

54. TRUE OR FALSE: THE DECLARATION OF INDEPENDENCE WAS WRITTEN ON ANIMAL SKIN.

True. This is partly why it has lasted so long, and in such good condition. Although some rumors state that it was written on hemp paper, these are false.

55. TRUE OR FALSE: THE TERM "RULE OF THUMB" COMES FROM AN OLD EDICT THAT A MAN COULD BEAT HIS WIFE, PROVIDED HE DID NOT USE A STICK THAT WAS WIDER THAN HIS THUMB.

False. Yet another long-perpetuated myth! Some references to this can be found throughout history, but only secondhand. No official pronouncement has ever been found, and it seems more likely that "rule of thumb" referred to planting depth among agriculturalists.

56. TRUE OR FALSE: BEFORE ITS DEMOLITION, THE KOWLOON WALLED CITY AREA OF HONG KONG WAS HOME TO OVER 30,000 PEOPLE IN JUST 0.01 SQUARE MILES OF SPACE.

True. The lawless region was home to extreme gang activity and heavy drug trafficking. It was demolished in 1993.

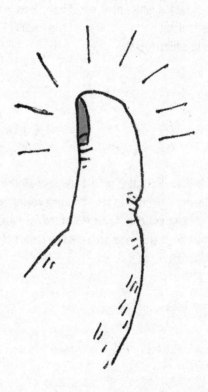

ABOUT THE AUTHOR

Shane Carley loves weird and unbelievable facts of all kinds, so when the opportunity came to write a fact book of his own, he took it. As a longtime science fiction aficionado, he acknowledges that the entire book might have been filled with space facts if not for the steady, guiding hand of the Cider Mill Press editorial staff.

ABOUT THE ILLUSTRATOR

Alex Kalomeris is an illustrator, printmaker, and all-around storyteller. His work revolves around creating narratives, characters, and impressions. Nautical, natural, and nostalgic themes show up in his work and are an integral part of his identity as an artist.